Oiga Por Favor

Rosa María Martín & Martyn Ellis

Hodder & Stoughton

LONDON SYDNEY AUCKLAND TORONTO

Acknowledgments

There are over 70 separate recorded Spanish voices on the accompanying cassette as well as many photographs of Spanish people at home, work and play. The authors would like to thank all those who willingly gave up their time to make such a valuable contribution to the material, especially the families Martín and Yuste.

Our special thanks also go to Bruce Colloff, who, with patience, skill and dedication in the sound studios, has retained the strong element of authenticity of the original bank of tapes in the final working version, and to our editor, Judith Brown, whose enthusiasm and helpful suggestions were a constant source of inspiration.

Thanks also to Sarah Cartwright, Co-ordinator of Modern Languages, and staff and students at Islington Sixth Form Centre in London whose open-minded approach and consistent support during the piloting of this material are greatly appreciated.

Lastly, thanks to the staff and students of Morley College, London where the material was also piloted.

The authors and publishers would like to thank the following for their kind permission to reproduce copyright material:

Cetesa and Telefonica for the use of symbols and a map from the Zaragoza telephone directory (pages 65, 66)
Iberia for the use of material from their emergency procedure brochure (page 32).
Direccion de Gestion Comercial for the train tickets reproduced on pages 25, 26.
Hotel Cueva del Fraille for the bill reproduced on page 41.
RTVE for permission to use (on cassette which accompanies this book) extracts from the programmes 'Todo queda en case'; 'Tocata'; 'La Tarde'; 'Consumo'; 'Suspiros de España'; and 'Agenda'.

Every effort has been made to trace copyright holders of material reproduced in this book. Any rights not acknowledged here will be acknowledged in subsequent printings if notice is given to the publisher.

British Library Cataloguing in Publication Data
Martin, R.M.
  Oiga, Por Favor.
  1. Spanish language—Text-books for
  foreign speakers—English
  I. Title II. Ellis, M.
  468 PC4112
  ISBN 0 7131 7619 9

First published 1988
Third impression 1990

© 1988 Rosa Maria Martin and Martyn Ellis

All rights reserved. No part of this publication may be reproduced or transmitted in any form or by any means, electronic or mechanical, including photocopy, recording, or any information storage and retrieval system, without permission in writing from the publisher or under licence from the Copyright Licensing Agency Limited. Further details of such licences (for reprographic reproduction) may be obtained from the Copyright Licensing Agency Limited, of 33–34 Alfred Place, London WC1E 7DP.

Printed in Great Britain for the educational publishing division of
Hodder and Stoughton Limited, Mill Road, Dunton Green, Sevenoaks, Kent
by Courier International Ltd, Tiptree, Essex.

Contents

Acknowledgments ii

Introduction iv

1 **Información personal** Giving/asking for personal details (age, birthplace, address, family); Describing physical appearance, character, personality; Likes/dislikes 1

2 **En el instituto** Describing daily school routines, classes, subjects, trips: Describing family relationships; Describing your room at home; Future plans (jobs, ambitions) 6

3 **Tiempo libre** Buying tickets (cinema, theatre, concert, disco, sport); Giving/accepting/declining an invitation; Deciding where to go; Describing your free time; Describing holidays 12

4 **El restaurant y el bar** Ordering meals and drinks; Complaining about food/service; Settling the bill; Describing eating habits and traditions 19

5 **Transporte público** Departure/arrival times (rail); Buying tickets; Travel accouncements; Asking for travel information; Checking in (airport); Customs procedure 25

6 **En la ciudad y en la carretera** Asking for information at the Tourist Office; Asking for/giving directions; Following a map; Tourist guide explanations; Hiring a car; At the garage (asking for petrol, arranging repairs); Problems on the road (phoning for help) 33

7 **El hotel y el apartamento** Booking in; Making a telephone reservation; Settling the bill; Complaints; Hotel rules; Renting an apartment 39

8 **En el camping y en la playa** Campsite facilities; Comparing campsites; Rules and regulations; Hiring beach equipment 45

9 **De compras** Shopping (food, general provisions, books and newspapers); Buying clothes in a department store; Store announcements; Exchanging damaged goods; Radio advertisements 52

10 **En el banco y en Correos** Changing traveller's cheques, cash; Bank transactions (opening an account); Post Office (sending mail, telegrams) 61

11 **Por teléfono** Making and receiving telephone calls; Leaving/taking messages; Telephone services (weather, time, sports); Reversing the charges 68

12 **En la comisaría** Reporting a theft; Describing lost/stolen property; Describing people; Police advice for tourists 74

13 **En el médico** Describing symptoms, illnesses; Giving advice, instructions, orders; Prescriptions; At the chemist; Making an appointment (doctor, dentist); Emergencies (casualty); Health in the summer holidays 80

14 **La radio y la televisión** Review 87

Introduction

This book, with its accompanying recorded material, is designed to meet the needs of students studying for the GCSE examination in Spanish, listening and speaking sections. Each of its 14 units deals with topic and vocabulary areas prescribed by the main examining boards. The units are subdivided into self-contained sections which provide realistic and authentic recordings of modern everyday Spanish through the voices of over 70 different speakers. These recordings are accompanied by a wide range of relevant and enjoyable comprehension tasks leading to guided speaking activities, many of which exploit the students' personal experiences and information. They are designed to develop confidence and communicative ability in the speaking skill. Comprehensive vocabulary lists at the end of each section combine useful words, phrases and idiomatic expressions in the context of the section which students are encouraged to study in their preparation for the speaking activities. Students studying for the Higher level of the examination are also directed towards the more complex material and related tasks indicated by the symbol **

The book follows a logical order and we advise you to adhere to this order where possible, although there is sufficient flexibility in the material to allow modification where appropriate. An accompanying guide of principle language areas in each unit appears in the Contents list.

All material has been thoroughly piloted both by school students at GCSE level and also by adult learners whose aim is to improve their listening and speaking skills in modern Spanish. Results so far have proved equally successful with both.

A companion volume, *Lea, por favor,* provides students with reading and writing practice on the same themes. The two books can be used together to form a comprehensive skills practice programme and vocabulary review.

RMM
ME

Información personal

A i Before you listen

Beatriz is joining a sports club. The secretary is asking for her name.
   What other information will she require?
   Practise questions in Spanish with your partner.

¿Cómo te llamas?
Beatriz Morales Yuste

A ii

Some of the information is missing from the enrolment card below. Listen to the dialogue between Beatriz and the secretary and complete the card with the missing information.

- When can she collect her membership card?

A iii

You will hear a student enrolling for an English course at a language school. Choose the correct answer for each of the following:

1 Name:
   a Yolanda
   b Lola
   c Ana

2 Address: Gonzalo de Berceo
   a 4, 5°, B
   b 4, 4°, B
   c 5, 4°, B

3 Age:
   a 16
   b 15
   c 14

4 Job:
   a office worker
   b typist
   c shop assistant

5 Come in for a test:
   a tomorrow afternoon
   b this afternoon
   c tomorrow morning

te espero en Inglaterra en las próximas vacaciones

International House
Escuela Internacional de Idiomas

STADIUM CASABLANCA

R- Aprobado en J. R. de ....
    Número de Registro ....

SOLICITUD SOCIO DE NUMERO

D. Beatriz Morales Yuste   con domicilio en calle Luis Braille

número .... piso .... Natural de ....   Fecha de nacimiento .... de .... de ....
Estado .... Profesión ....   (indicar centro estudios, organismo o empresa
donde trabaja) ....   Hijo de ....   profesión ....
y de .... profesión ....   domiciliados en ....

Oiga, por favor

A iv **Role play**

Listen to dialogue Aiii and then practise a similar role play with a partner, taking turns to be the secretary and the student. The secretary needs the following information:

1 Surname (he/she might want you to spell it).
2 Address
3 Age
4 Job
5 When can you do the test?

A v

You will hear five short dialogues in which people are talking about their age and birthday. Find the information missing below. Use Vocabulary A to help you.

	Años	Cumpleaños
1 Ana	12	
2 José Luis		26 – 3
3 Mari Carmen		
4 Javier		
5 Alicia		

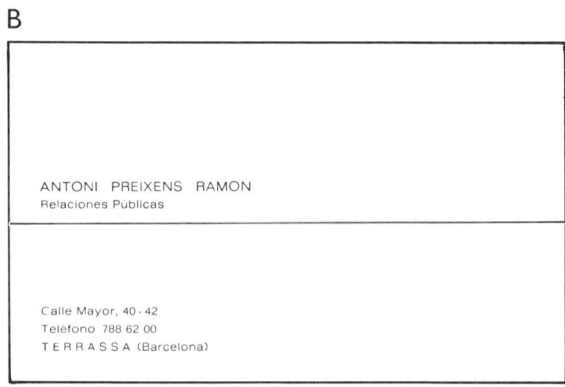

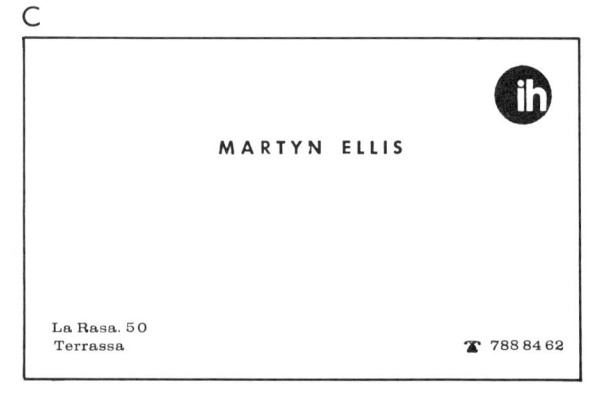

A vi

You will hear four people giving information about their professions. Look at the four incomplete business cards and write down the names of the profession or position missing from three of the four cards.

A

M.ª PILAR GONZALEZ MARTINEZ-PARDO

Avda. Goya, 16-18, 1.º D
Teléfono 21 20 95   ZARAGOZA-6

B

ANTONI PREIXENS RAMON
Relaciones Públicas

Calle Mayor, 40 - 42
Teléfono 788 62 00
TERRASSA (Barcelona)

C

ih

MARTYN ELLIS

La Rasa, 50
Terrassa   ☎ 788 84 62

Información personal

D

LUIS FALCON

Reina Fabiola, 26 :•: Teléfono 41 69 68 :•: ZARAGOZA - 8

A vii**

Now listen to speakers 1 and 4 again and answer these questions.

1 What is speaker 1 doing at the moment?
2 What is speaker 4 doing at the moment?

vocabulary A

Vengo a hacerme socio	I've come to join
apuntarme	to join/to enrol
¿Cómo te llamas?	What's your name?
¿Cómo se llama?	What's your name/What's his/her name
Me llamo...	I'm/my name is
soltero/a	single
Vamos a rellenar esta ficha	We'll just complete this form
¿Dónde vives?	Where do you live?
domicilio/dirección (f)	address
Vivo...	I live...
¿De dónde eres/es?	Where are you from?
¿Eres/Es de aquí?	Are you from here?
¿Cuándo naciste/nació?	When were you born?
¿Cuántos años tiene(s)?	How old are you?
edad (f)	age
Tengo dieciséis años	I'm sixteen
¿Cuándo es tu cumpleaños?	When is your birthday?
¿En qué trabajas?	What do you work at?
¿Cuál es tu profesión?	What is your job?
¿Estudias?	Do you study?
Soy/Es mecánico	I'm/He/She is a mechanic
ama de casa	housewife
profesor/a	teacher
estudiante	student
dependiente/a	shop assistant
secretario/a	secretary/office worker
licenciado/a en Filosofía y Letras	graduate of Philosophy and letters
mecanógrafo/a	typist
camarero/a	waiter/waitress
Relaciones Públicas	public relations (officer)
Trabajo en un banco	I work in a bank
una papelería	a stationer's
una tienda	a shop
director de una escuela de Idiomas	director of a language school
ahora	now
Estoy haciendo el servicio militar	I'm doing my military service
Estoy en paro	I'm unemployed
4°/cuarto	fourth floor
6°/sexto	sixth floor
9°/noveno	ninth floor
mañana por la mañana	tomorrow morning

Oiga, por favor

B i**

You will hear four people (nos. 1–4 below) talking about themselves and their families. As you listen, choose from the options below the correct personal details for each speaker. Marisol's details have already been done for you.

1 = Marisol
2 = Antonio
3 = Pilar
4 = Domingo

Lugar de nacimiento	Sant Cugat (del Vallés)	Belchite	Sabadell	Cádiz
Fecha de nacimiento	5 de septiembre	doesn't say	5 de noviembre	11 de septiembre
Edad	54	25	16	doesn't say
Profesión	dependiente/a	estudiante	ferroviario	guardia urbano
Hermanos	1 hermana menor	1 hermano menor	1 hermano mayor	doesn't say
Hijos	1 hijo	2 hijos	ninguno	1 hijo

B ii Speaking practice

Look at the headings in Bi and make questions to ask for each item of information. For example, to obtain the information *Lugar de nacimiento*, you need the question *¿Dónde naciste?* In pairs find out this information about each other.

B iii**

Look at the photograph of a Spanish family. You will hear somebody describing each member of the family. Indicate in which order they are mentioned.

B iv Speaking practice

Bring in photographs of your own family and do the same as in Biii.

Información personal

vocabulary B

ferrocarril (m)	railway	madre	mother
ferroviario	railway worker	alto/a	tall
guardia urbano (m)	traffic policeman/woman	bajo/a	short
comercio	shop/store	delgado/a	thin
instituto	secondary school	gordo/a	fat
BUP (Bachillerato Unificado Polivalente)	secondary school studies (baccalaureat)	simpático/a	kind, nice
		agradable	pleasant
anciano/a	elderly person	antipático/a	unpleasant, unfriendly
hermano/a	brother/sister	tonto/a	stupid
hijo/a	son/daughter	inteligente	intelligent
nieto/a	grandson/granddaughter	normal	normal/average
primo/a	cousin	castaño/a	brown (for hair)
cuñado/a	brother-in-law/sister-in-law	rubio/a	fair/blonde
tío/a	uncle/aunt	moreno/a	dark
marido	husband	deportistas	sportsmen/women
sobrino/a	nephew/niece	bonito/a	pretty
abuelo/a	grandfather/grandmother	apariencia física	physical appearance
niño/a	child	ojos azules (m)	blue eyes

C ¡**

You will hear Ma Carmen talking about boys and Antonio talking about girls. Write down:

1 Two things Ma Carmen likes in a boy.

   a) Physical appearance: _____

   b) Character: _____

2 Two things she dislikes.

3 Two things Antonio likes in a girl.

   a) Physical appearance: _____

   b) Character: _____

4 Two things he dislikes.

D ¡**

You will hear part of a television programme called 'Suspiros de España'. In it, ordinary Spanish people are invited to talk about anything they like. Answer the questions below for the four people interviewed.

1 a) What does José Manuel want?

   b) Where can you write to him?

   c) Where does his friend work?

   d) What is his phone number?

2 a) Where is Alejandro from?

   b) Where is he spending his holiday?

   c) How often does he go to Spain?

   d) How does he feel about being in Spain?

3 a) How many children does Esmeralda have?

   b) What does the family live on?

   c) What does she want for her town?

T V E
Martes 3
Segunda Cadena

18,45. — **Carta de ajuste.**
19,00. — **Agenda.**
19,15. — **En marcha.**
19,30. — **Niels Holgersson.**
20,00. — **Tiempos modernos.**
21,00. — **Coraje.**
21,30. — **Suspiros de España.**
22,00. — **La duna móvil:** «Doñana».
23,00. — **Pushkin y su obra.**
 0,10. — **Las rutas vikingas.**
 0,40. — **Telediario.**
 1,10. — **Despedida y cierre.**

En el instituto 2

A i Before you listen

Yolanda is talking about her school and her studies. What questions might you want to ask her?

Practise questions in Spanish with a partner.

A ii

Listen to Yolanda and answer the following questions:

1. How old is she?
2. What course is she studying?
3. Look at the list of school subjects below. Which ones does Yolanda mention?

- biology ☐
- chemistry ☐
- physics ☐
- maths ☐
- Spanish language ☐
- English ☐
- French ☐
- literature ☐
- social studies ☐
- ethics ☐
- history ☐
- geography ☐
- music ☐
- sport ☐

A iii

You will hear four young people describing their school studies. Copy the table below and from the information on the tape:

a) indicate their age
b) indicate which course of study they are doing and which year they are in. (COU is one year only.)

	Age	EGB	BUP	COU
Anna Rosa	16		2	
Manolo				
Domi				
Ana				

A iv

Now listen to the recording again and decide which of the subjects below are mentioned by each person. (Some of the ones they mention are not listed.)

a) English   d) Latin   g) gymnastics
b) French   e) history   h) religion
c) Greek   f) geography i) literature

En el instituto

A v Speaking practice

In pairs or groups, state your name, age, your year at school and some of the subjects you study. (Use the vocabulary list to help you.)

Which are your favourite subjects? Which are your least favourite subjects? Give reasons. Which subjects are you going to do next year?

vocabulary A

los estudios	studies
¿Qué estudias?	What do you study?
Estudio...	I study...
He acabado octavo de EGB	I've finished the eighth year of EGB
EGB (Educación General Básica)	General Basic Education
BUP (Bachillerato Unificado Polivalente)	Baccalaureate
COU (Curso de Orientación Universitaria)	University entrance course
asignatura	school subject
física	physics
química	chemistry
matemáticas	mathematics
ciencias sociales	social sciences
ciencias puras	science
ciencias naturales	Natural science
letras	Arts
biología	biology
lengua (Española)	language/Spanish
lenguaje (m)	language (Spanish)
idiomas (m)	languages
inglés (m)	English
francés (m)	French
catalán (m)	Catalan
griego	Greek
latín (m)	Latin
filosofía	Philosophy
ética	Ethics
música	music
historia	history
literatura	literature
religión (f)	religion
gimnasia	gymnastics
deportes (m)	sports
optativo/a	optional
obligatorio/a	compulsory
colegio	school
instituto	secondary school
alumno/a	pupil
estudiante	student

B i

You will hear Ana Rosa describing her 'instituto', her teachers and the subjects she studies.

What can you say about the following?

1. The time it takes her to get to school.
2. The number of hours she spends at school.
3. Which afternoon she has free.
4. Her favourite subjects.
5. Her least favourite subjects
6. The size of the classrooms.
7. The state of the classrooms.
8. The age of the building.
9. The number of students per class.
10. The relationship between students and teachers.

Oiga, por favor

B ii Speaking practice

Work in pairs.

1 Ask and answer the questions below in Spanish:
   a) Ask your partner how long it takes to get to school.
   b) Ask how many hours he/she has to study each day.
   c) Ask about school subjects.
   d) Ask him/her to describe the school.
   e) Ask another question.

** In pairs discuss what subjects you would like to do in your school which are not offered at the moment. What changes would you like to see?

B iii

You will hear Domi and his father Domingo describing a typical day in their lives.

1 Copy the chart below and put the correct times in the boxes (where applicable).

	Domi	Domingo
Get up		
Start the day		
Back for lunch		
Start the afternoon		
Finish the day		

2 How do they spend their free time?

B iv Speaking practice

Work in pairs. Describe to your partner a typical day. Ask each other questions.

---

vocabulary B

profesor/a	teacher
clase (f)	class/classroom
fiesta	holiday, day off
horario	timetable
Cansa mucho	It's very tiring
agotador	exhausting
mecanografía	typing
informática	computer studies
aprobar un examen	to pass an exam
suspender un examen	to fail an exam
carrera	university course
Me levanto a las ocho	I get up at eight
Desayuno/Almuerzo	I have breakfast
comer	to eat
entrar al colegio	start school/get to school
entrar al trabajo	start work/get to work
hacer la jornada	do the day's work
salir del colegio/del trabajo	leave school/work
dar un paseo	go out for a walk
pasear por el campo	walk in the countryside
un descanso	a break, a rest
descansar un rato	relax for a while
arreglar alguna cosa	repair something

En el instituto

C i

You will hear three people describing themselves.
Copy the chart below and write down one or two things in each column for each person. (Yolanda says nothing about her physical appearance.)

	Personality	Physical Appearance
1	Ana Rosa	
2	Manolo	
3	Yolanda	

C ii **

Now you will hear Yolanda and Ana Rosa describing their families and their relationships with their brothers, sisters and parents.
Look at the choices below and match the statements to the speakers.

1. a) gets on with brother/sister well
   b) gets on with brother/sister reasonably
   c) gets on with brother/sister badly
2. a) gets on with father well
   b) gets on with father reasonably
   c) gets on with father badly
3. a) gets on with mother well
   b) gets on with mother reasonably
   c) gets on with mother badly

C iii** Speaking practice

In pairs or groups describe the rest of your family to each other. How do you get on with your brothers and sisters and your parents? Ask each other questions.

vocabulary C

cerrado/a	reserved	Tengo apariencia normal	I have a normal/average appearance
abierto/a	open	engreído/a	conceited
tímido/a	shy		
serio/a	serious	¿Qué tal te llevas con tu hermano?	How do you get on with your brother?
discutir	to argue		
reñir/pelear	to bicker, fight	Me llevo bien/mal/regular con él	I get on well/badly/all right with him
me cuesta hacer amigos	I find it difficult to make friends	No nos llevamos muy bien	We don't get on very well
(no) me adapto a la persona	I (can't) adapt to the person	Me dejan salir	They let me go out
		No me dicen nada (si voy a las diez)	They don't say anything (if I go (get home) at 10 o'clock)
mayor que	older than		
el/la mayor	the oldest		

Oiga, por favor

D i

You will hear Ana Rosa, Yolanda and Manolo describing their bedrooms. For each room make simple drawings of the things they describe. For example:

When you have listened to all three descriptions, compare your sketches with your partner's and check to see if you have missed anything.

vocabulary D

cuarto	room	cosas colgadas	hanging things
habitación (f)	room	cuadro	picture
cama	bed	decorado/a	decorated
armario	wardrobe	mesilla/mesita de noche	bedside table
mesa	table	mi propio/a	my own
sillón (m)	armchair	empapelado	wallpapered
escritorio	desk	da/orientado al paseo	it gives onto the street
estanterías	shelves	pasillo	corridor/hallway
muñeco/muñeca	doll	lavabo	washbasin
figura	ornamental figure	armario empotrado	fitted wardrobe
posters (m)	posters	equipo de música	stereo system

D ii Speaking practice

Now, in pairs, describe your room to your partner who should make a sketch of what you describe. Check that he/she has included everything.

E i**

Manolo talks about his spare time jobs and money. Decide whether each of the following statements is true or false:

1 Manolo works in an office in his spare time.
2 He has a savings account in the bank.
3 He gets most of his money from his parents.
4 He buys his own clothes with the money he earns.
5 He spends most of his money on records.

Información personal

📼 E ii**

Javier talks about his future plans and ambitions. Answer the following questions:

1. What is he studying at the moment?
2. Is he optimistic about the future?
3. What two possibilities does he think he has?
4. What would he most like to do?

📼 Fi** Viajes de Estudio

You will hear two recordings of Manolo and Yolanda describing 'Viajes de Estudio'.

1. Listen to both recordings and give a definition of 'Viajes de Estudio'.
2. Copy the chart below. Now listen again and fill in the details.

	Yolanda	Manolo
Duration		
Places visited		
When?		
Accommodation		
How they collected money		
What they did		
Transport		

📼 E iii**

Rafa and Manolo talk about pets and helping around the house. Answer the following questions:

1. Have they got any pets now?
2. Name two pets they used to have.
4. How do they help around the house?

Tiempo libre

A i Before you listen

Look at the photograph. A woman is asking about tickets at the cinema. What is her question? What other information might she want?

Practise questions in Spanish with your partner.

A ii

Listen to the dialogue and answer the following questions:

1. What time does the performance start?
2. How many tickets does she want?
3. Are the seats numbered?
4. Where are the seats?
5. What is the price of the ticket?

A iii

You will hear 3 people buying tickets for different kinds of events. Copy the chart below and complete the gaps with the relevant information.

	Discotheque	Bullfight	Football
No of tickets			
Type of ticket			
Starting time			
Finishing time			

Tiempo libre

A iv

In each of the six recorded statements you will hear a ticket seller explaining why the customer cannot have the tickets he/she has asked for. An alternative will also be offered.

Answer the following questions for each situation. The first one is done for you.

A   Where does the person want to go?
    1   the cinema
B   What is the problem?
    1   no seats for 9 p.m.
C   What alternative is offered?
    1   seats for 11 p.m.

A v Role plays

Act out the following role plays in pairs. In each case A is the customer and B is the ticket seller.

At the cinema:

1   A: Ask what time the film starts.
    B: The next performance is at 7 p.m.
    A: Ask if there are later performances.
    B: There are performances at 9 and 10.45.
    A: Ask how much the tickets cost.
    B: 300 pesetas.
    A: Ask if there are tickets for the 9 p.m. performance
    B: There are some but not many.
    A: Ask for two.

2   A: You want two tickets for tonight's 9 p.m. performance.
    B: There aren't any tickets for tonight.
    A: Ask if you can book for tomorrow.
    B: Yes, Which performance?
    A: Decide – 5, 7, 9 or 10.45.

3   A: You want two tickets for this performance.
    B: There aren't any left for this performance.
    A: Are there any for the 9 p.m. performance?
    B: Yes, there are, but not many.
    A: Ask for two at 300 pts.
    B: There are only 400 pts tickets left.
    A: Decide whether you want them or not.

At the theatre

1   A: Ask the price of the cheapest seats.
    B: 600 pts.
    A: Which part of the theatre is that?
    B: Very high at the back.
    A: Ask for something a bit nearer the stage.
    B: Offer a seat at 800 pts.
    A: Ask for two.

Oiga, por favor

2** A: You have two tickets for tonight's performance but your friend can't go. Can they sell it for you?
B: Apologise but you cannot do that.
A: Ask what you can do.
B: Suggest trying to sell the ticket as people come in for tickets, as there are no tickets left at the box office.
A: Thank him/her.

At the concert hall

1** A: You have a ticket for Friday night's performance. Can you change it for Saturday night?
B: The only seats left for Saturday are at 1200 pts. The customer's ticket is for 900 pts.
A: Say you will pay the extra.

2 A: Ask for two tickets at 1000 pts.
B: Which part of the concert hall does he/she want the seat in?
A: Choose stalls (*butaca*) near the front.
B: Offer the fifth row.
A: That's perfect.

vocabulary A

¿Hay entradas/localidades?	Are there any tickets/seats?	discoteca	discotheque
en un buen sitio	in a good place	concierto	concert
No hay localidades	There are no seats left	consumición (*f*)	drinks
¿Son numeradas?	Are they numbered?	corrida	bullfight
para la sesión de las siete.	for the seven o'clock performance	sol/sombra	sun/shade (choice of seat at a bullfight)
taquilla	box office	campo de fútbol	football ground
butaca	stalls	partido de fútbol	football match
fila	row	general de pie	terraces for standing at a football match
de atrás	at the back		
de delante	at the front	pista de hielo	skating rink
¿Cuanto dura?	How long does it last?	patinar	to skate
La sesión empieza/termina a las siete	The performance starts/finishes at seven	venta anticipada	advanced sales
		socio/a	member
madrugada	early hours of the morning	piscina municipal	municipal swimming pool
		pista de circo	circus ring
No me quedan entradas	I haven't any tickets left	devolver el importe	give money back
Me quedan pocas	I only have a few left	Se ha suspendido la función	The event has been called off
Me quedan algunas	I have a few left		
obra (de teatro)	play		

B i

You will hear Javier inviting a friend to the cinema. Look at the details of the three films below and:

1 Decide which one they decide to see.
2 Give two reasons why they don't want to see the other two.
3 Say what time they decide to go.
4 Say where they will meet.

Minicines Majadahonda. Sala 1.
☎ 638 08 87 / Zoco Majadahonda.
—**Psicosis III.** Laborables: 6.15, 8.30 y 10.15. Sábado y domingo, también 4.15.

Coliseum. (3) / ☎ 247 66 12 / Gran Vía, 78; Centro / *Metro* Plaza de España.
—**Rocky.** ¡Vuelve Rocky! ¡Luchó hasta el límite de sus fuerzas! 4.30, 7 y 10.

Capitol. (4) / ☎ 222 22 29 / Gran Vía, 41; Centro / *Metro* Callao.
—**Aliens.** 4.15, 7.15 y 10.15. No recomendada a menores de 13 años.

B ii

You will hear short descriptions of five types of film. From the list below:

1 Select the ones which are mentioned on the tape.
2 Decide the order in which they are mentioned.

a) horror
b) comedy
c) science fiction
d) police thriller
e) western
f) cartoon
g) musical
h) adventure

B iii

You will hear two people discussing which television programme to watch. Answer the questions below:

1 What does Yolanda want to watch?
2 What does Javier want to watch?
3 What do they decide?

B iv

Now the same two people are discussing how to spend an evening out together. You will hear them expressing likes and dislikes.

1 Copy and complete the chart at the foot of this page, using a tick for 'likes' and a cross for 'dislikes'.
2 Where do they decide to go?

B v

You will hear two friends, Mari Carmen and Curro, making a date to go out. Look at Mari Carmen's diary below. Some of her arrangements for the week are already filled in. Make a note of the other days and times when she is busy.

Which is the only time she is free to go out?

NOVIEMBRE	NOVIEMBRE
Lunes 3 Clases todo el día 6 - Dentista Deberes	Jueves 6 Clases todo el día
Martes 4 Clases - mañana 9-1	Viernes 7 Clases 9-1
Miércoles 5 Clases 9-1	Sábado 8
	Domingo 9

	discotheque	restaurant	theatre	ice-skating	cinema
Yolanda					
Javier					

B vi Role play

1 Act out the following role play in pairs:

A: Say there is a good horror film on at the cinema this evening and invite your friend to see it.

B: You would like to go to the cinema but you don't like horror films.

A: Ask if he/she likes thrillers. There is a good thriller at a cinema nearby.

B: Ask if it's violent. You don't like too much violence.

A: You don't think it's very violent.

B: Agree to go.

2 Invent further role plays like the above, using the vocabulary below to help you.

vocabulary B

Ponen/Echan una película de terror	They are showing a horror film	Telediario	Spanish television news programme
sacar las entradas	to buy the tickets (for a cinema etc.)	deporte (m)	sport
el musical	musical	atletismo	athletics
estupendo	wonderful, great	ópera	opera
Está muy bien	It's very good	aburrido/a	boring
Da mucho miedo	It's very frightening	divertido/a	enjoyable
complicado/a	complicated	Me aburro	I'm bored
asesino	the murderer	Me duele	It hurts me
viajes (m) espaciales	space journeys	Me torcí el tobillo	I twisted my ankle
bailar	to dance	¿Qué te parece...?	How about...?
¿Te apetece?	Do you feel like it?	Estoy muy ocupado/a	I'm very busy
¿Te gustaría?	Would you like to?	Estoy libre	I'm free
Me gustaría ir/entrar	I'd like to go/go in	ir de compras	to go shopping
Me encantaría	I'd love to	Hasta entonces	Until then
Me gusta/No me gusta esquiar	I like/I don't like skiing	Vale	O.K.
		De acuerdo	All right
Poner la tele	To put the television on	deberes (m)	homework
la cadena	channel	Quedamos en la entrada a las siete	We'll meet at the entrance at seven
noticias	the news	¿Te va bien?	Is that O.K. with you?

C i

You will hear three different people (Manolo, Javier and Ana-Rosa) describing how they spend their free time. Look at the list of activities below and for each speaker choose the relevant activities.

a) rock music
b) pop music
c) classical music
d) discotheque (dancing)
e) basketball
f) tennis
g) skiing
h) cinema
i) theatre
j) going for walks
k) television
l) reading

Tiempo libre

C ii Speaking practice

Work in groups. Describe what you like doing in your free time, in Spanish. Ask each other questions.

vocabulary C

oír	to hear/listen to	días de fiesta	holidays, weekends, days off
música fuerte	loud heavy/rock music	ver la tele	to watch the television
rock (m)	rock music	leer libros	to read books
música clásica	classical music	películas de aventura	adventure films
pop	pop	misterio	mystery
moderna	modern	intriga	intrigue
estudios	studies	risa	comedy
dar una vuelta	to go for a walk	humor	comedy
conocer gente	to meet people	Vamos a misa	We go to Mass
baloncesto	basketball	Vamos a tomar algo	We go out for a drink
jugar al tenis	to play tennis		

D i**

In Spain schoolchildren spend 10 or 15 days in what is known as 'Campamento', a sort of school holiday. You will hear Yolanda describing a typical day.

1 Look at the timetable opposite. As you listen, make a note of the missing information.

9.00 – Levantarse

10.00 – _____

10.30 – Arreglar habitación

11.00 – _____

2.00 – Ducha

2.30 – _____

3.30 – _____

4.30 – Actividades

6.00 – Merienda

9.30 – _____

2 What are three of the things they used to do in their activity time?

3 What did they do in the evening after supper?

D ii**

You will hear Rosa showing her friend some photos which she took on holiday. The photos are shown below. Decide in which order she talks about them.

D iii** Speaking practice

Bring some photos of your holidays and describe them to your partner in Spanish.

El restaurante y el bar 4

A i Before you listen

1 Think of some of the things you can eat and drink in a restaurant. Make a list in Spanish.

2 In the photographs, what is the waiter saying to the woman? What is she saying to him?

¿Qué van a tomar de primer plato?

Para mí, sopa.

A ii

You will hear a man and a woman ordering a meal in a restaurant. Copy the chart below and complete it. The first item has been done for you.

	El señor		*La señora*	
Primer plato	Ensalada	☐	Ensalada	☐
	Sopa	☐	Sopa	☑
	Zumo de tomate	☐	Zumo de tomate	☐
Segundo plato	Pollo a la chilindrón	☐	Pollo a la chilindrón	☐
	Lomo con tomate	☐	Lomo con tomate	☐
	Merluza a la romana	☐	Merluza a la romana	☐
Postre	Helado	☐	Helado	☐
	Flan	☐	Flan	☐
	Fruta del tiempo	☐	Fruta del tiempo	☐

Oiga, por favor

A iii**

Look at the pictures below. With a partner decide what is being said, in Spanish, in each picture.

Listen to the six extracts and match each one with the appropriate picture. Were your original answers similar to what is on the tape?

A

B

C

D

E

F

El restaurant y el bar

A iv**

You will hear two people ordering a meal from the menu below. Using the menu to help you, write down the answers to the questions that follow.

Menú

PRIMER PLATO

Ensaladilla rusa
Ensalada mixta
Berenjenas rellenas
Sopa de pollo
Sopa de pescado
Zumo de tomate
Entremeses
Menestra de verduras

SEGUNDO PLATO

Pollo al ajillo
Pollo a la chilindrón
Chuleta de ternera
Conejo con mayonesa
Bistec a la pimienta
Merluza a la vasca
Trucha a la navarra
Estofado de ternera

POSTRE

Melocotón en almibar
Flan
Helados variados
Helado de la casa
Fruta
Tarta de whisky

BEBIDAS

Vino tinto *de la casa*
Vino blanco
Clarete

Cerveza
Agua mineral con gas
                  sin gas

Zumos

1. What does the woman order for the first course?
2. What does the waiter recommend for the second course?
3. Why doesn't the man order what is recommended?
4. Which dish is the waiter unable to offer?
5. What is the man's final choice?
6. What kind of wine do they order?
7. Who does *not* order a sweet?
8. Do they both order white coffee?
9. What is the waiter's mistake?

A v Role play

Act out the following role plays in pairs. In each case, A is the waiter and B is the customer.

1. A: Ask what he/she wants for the first course.
   B: Choose something from the menu.
   A: Ask what the customer wants for the second course.
   B: Ask the waiter to recommend something.
   A: Recommend something.
   B: Order this recommendation.
   A: Ask what the customer wants to drink.
   B: Order something non-alcoholic.

2. The customer has finished the main course.
   A: Ask what the customer wants for dessert.
   B: Ask what 'tarta de whisky' is like.
   A: Describe it (cake with ice cream and whisky).
   B: You prefer ice cream. Order it.
   A: Ask if the customer will be having coffee.
   B: Order black coffee.

3.** Before starting this role play, the customer should look at the menu and decide what he/she wants for the first two courses.
   A: Ask the customer to order.
   B: Order the first two courses.
   A: You haven't got whatever the customer wants for the main (second) course. Recommend an alternative.
   B: Accept the recommendation or choose something different.
   A: Ask what he/she wants to drink.
   B: Order something to drink.

4. Practise the continuation of no. 3. The customer must order a sweet and coffee and then ask for the bill.

Oiga, por favor

vocabulary A

¿Qué va/van a tomar? ¿Qué tomarán? ¿Qué quiere(n) tomar?	What will you have
... de primero	for the first course
... de postre	for dessert
Yo quiero/Tomaré ...	I'll have ...
Tráigame ...	Bring me ...
Para mí el menú del día	For me the menu of the day
Qué me recomienda?	What do you recommend?
Le recomiendo ...	I recommend
sopa	soup
ensalada	salad
bistec (m) a la pimienta	steak with peppers
chuleta de ternera	veal chop
pollo (a la chilindrón)	chicken (cooked in a special style)
frito con { pimiento, tomate (m), cebolla, jamón serrano (m) }	fried with { pepper, tomato, onion, smoked ham }
conejo con mayonesa	rabbit with mayonnaise
lomo	pork
merluza	hake
bien hecho	well done
entremeses (m)	hors d'oeuvres
menestra de verduras	mixed fried vegetables
trucha a la navarra	trout (Navarran style)
patatas fritas	chips
flan	cream caramel
helado	ice cream
fruta del tiempo	fruit (of the season)
naranja	orange
plátano	banana
melocotón	peach
¿Para beber?	To drink?
vino de la casa	house wine
vino tinto	red wine
agua con/sin gas	sparkling/still water
café solo	black coffee
café con leche	white coffee
cortado	small coffee with little milk
Quédese con el cambio	Keep the change
Tráiganos la cuenta	Bring us the bill

B i**

You will hear six short dialogues (a–f) in each of which something is wrong with the bill. Decide what is wrong in each case. The first is done for you.

a) *This is the wrong bill.*

B ii Role play**

Look at the following bills. Each is wrong in some way. Bring the mistake to the attention of the waiter. What will the waiter say in response?

1
```
2 ensalada    400
2 pollo       950
2 aguas        70
2 pan          40
2 helado      200
             1660
```
You ordered pork.

2
```
2 ensalada    400
2 chuletas    850
  vino tinto  100
2 pan          40
2 flan        150
             1640
```
Wrong total.

3
```
2 sopa        300
2 conejo      900
2 patatas     100
2 cerveza     100
1 helado       60
1 fruta        50
             1510
```
You didn't order chips.

4
```
2 ensalada    400
2 chuletas    850
  vino 'Banda
      Azul'   220
2 pan          40
2 flan        150
             1660
```
You ordered house wine, which is cheaper. This is a brand wine.

5
```
2 sopa        300
2 conejo      900
2 patatas     100
2 agua         70
2 helado      120
             1490
```
Wrong bill.

El restaurant y el bar

vocabulary B

La cuenta está equivocada	The bill is wrong
El total está mal	The total is wrong
Lo he sumado mal	I've added it up wrongly
Ésta no es mi comida	This isn't my meal
Esta cuenta no es la nuestra	This bill isn't ours
Tiene razón	You're right
He/hemos tomado . . .	I/We had . . .
Me/Nos ha traido lomo	You brought me/us pork
Aquí pone 500 pesetas	It says here 500 pesetas
Nos ha cobrado dos	You have charged us for two
Hace rato que pedimos	We ordered some time ago

C i

Copy the chart below.
You will hear five short dialogues in which a customer is ordering and paying. Complete the chart from the information on the tape.

	Beber	Comer	Total
1			
2			
3			
4			
5			

C ii Role play

1 Now use the recording in Ci and Vocabulary C to help you reproduce the same dialogues in pairs.

2 Make similar dialogues in pairs using the price list in Ci.

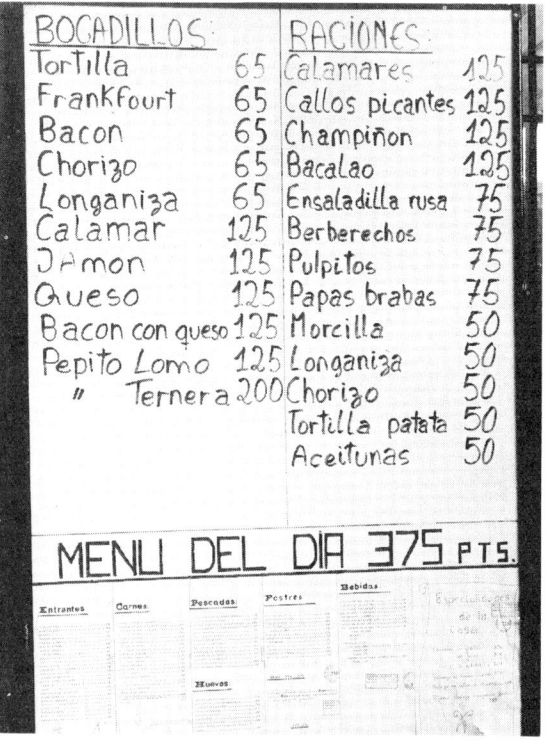

BOCADILLOS:

Tortilla	65
Frankfourt	65
Bacon	65
Chorizo	65
Longaniza	65
Calamar	125
Jamon	125
Queso	125
Bacon con queso	125
Pepito Lomo	125
" Ternera	200

RACIONES:

Calamares	125
Callos picantes	125
Champiñon	125
Bacalao	125
Ensaladilla rusa	75
Berberechos	75
Pulpitos	75
Papas brabas	75
Morcilla	50
Longaniza	50
Chorizo	50
Tortilla patata	50
Aceitunas	50

MENU DEL DIA 375 PTS.

Entrantes   Carnes   Pescados   Postres   Bebidas

Oiga, por favor

vocabulary C

¿Qué le/les pongo	What would you like? (formal)	un bocadillo de jamón	a ham sandwich in French bread
¿Qué te/os pongo?	What would you like? (familiar)	una cerveza	a beer
¿Me pone . . . ?	Could you give me . . . ?	una sidra	a cider
¿Puede darme . . . ?	Could you give me . . . ?	un refresco	a soft drink
Póngame/Ponme . . .	Give me . . .	un zumo de naranja	an orange juice
una tapa	snack	una naranjada	an orange drink
una ración de . . .	a portion of . . .	¿Qué te/le debo?	What do I owe you?
calamares (m)	squid	¿Puede(s) cobrarme?	Could you take for this?
patatas fritas	crisps/chips	¿Me/Nos cobra?	
una ensaladilla	a Russian salad	En seguida	Right away

D i**

You will hear part of a radio programme called 'Un menú para hoy'. Listen and answer the following questions:

1 What season of the year is it?
2 What type of food do people prefer at this time of year?
3 What is suggested as an aperitif?
4 Why should you avoid spicy food?
5 What is recommended for the second course?
6 What is recommended for stuffing?
7 What is important about the sweet?
8 How long will the sweet take to make?

D ii

Spanish people have six names for possible meals and snacks which can be taken at different times of the day. Look at the list below and try to put them in the correct order. Also put approximate times next to each.

a) la merienda   d) el almuerzo
b) el desayuno   e) la cena
c) la comida   f) el aperitivo

Now listen to the tape and check the order. Did you get the times right?

Listen again and write down one or two items of food and/or drink for each meal or snack mentioned on the tape.

D iii Role play

Work in pairs. One of you should take the role of a Spanish person asking about eating habits in your country and how they compare to those in Spain.

The questioner should find out the following:

   what time most people have breakfast.
   what they have for breakfast.
   what time they have lunch.
   where they have lunch.
   what they have for lunch.
   what is the main meal of the day.
   what time the evening meal is eaten.
   what it consists of.
   if there are any other eating habits not mentioned.

Transporte público 5

A i Before you listen

Buenos días ¿Qué desea?

Un billete para Madrid, por favor

Look at the picture taken at a station ticket office. What does the woman want? What other information will the ticket seller need?

Practise questions and answers in Spanish with your partner.

A ii

Now listen to the entire conversation and answer the following questions:

1. How many trains are there to Madrid this afternoon?
2. Which one does she decide to take?
3. When does the woman want to return?
4. Does she smoke?
5. How much does the ticket cost?

A iii

Look at the two train tickets below and study the information given on them. Some of it is missing. Listen to the two dialogues and add the missing information.

1

RENFE EXPEDICION ELECTRONICA	NO ES VALIDO PARA EL REGRESO SIN LA PREVIA FORMALIZACION EN TAQUILLA		BILLETE DE IDA Y VUELTA		A 804018	VIAJES	

Entréguese al finalizar el viaje de regreso

	VIAJE DE IDA							FORMALIZACION DEL VIAJE DE VUELTA
NUM. DE TREN	FECHA	CLASE	NUM. DE COCHE	ASIENTO	HORA DE SALIDA	TARIFA	PRECIO PTS.	Tren n.° 170 del día 10/03/1984 Sello de la dependencia
TALGO	?	2	022	016	?	13	?	

57011105037100170010030000216509100 1.

01650813128410804 6661 IDA Y VUELTA
                        DESDE   HASTA

NUM. DE CONTROL FUMADOR   ZARAGOZA CHM A   ?

Léase el dorso

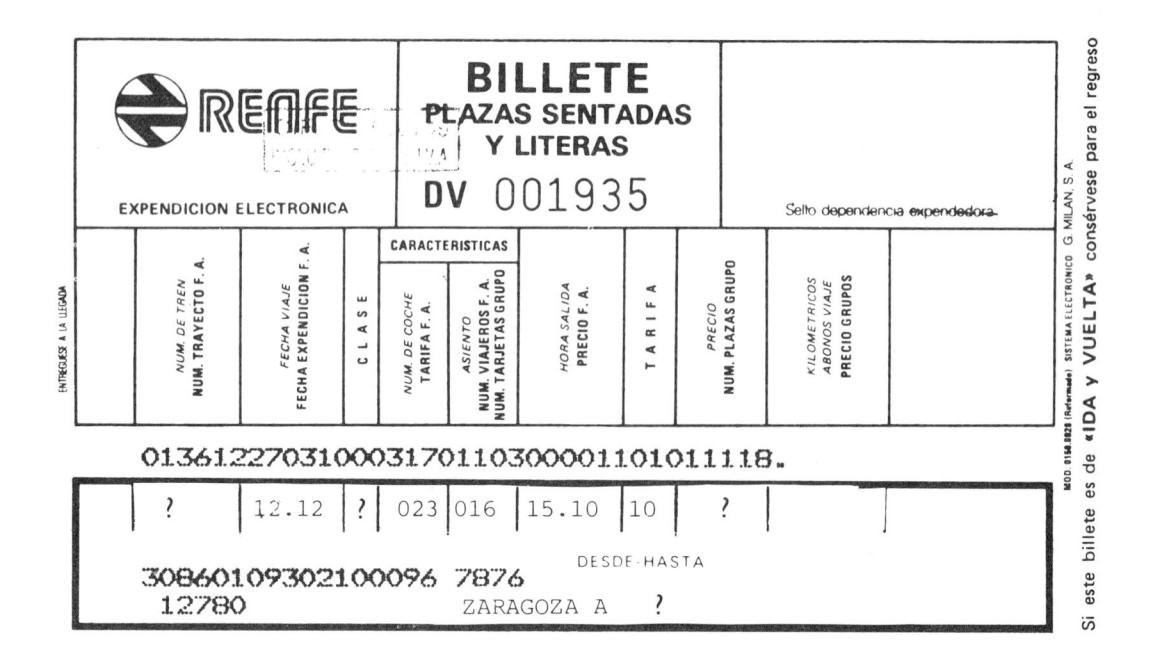

A iv **Role play**

In pairs, act out the following role plays between a ticket seller (A) and a passenger (B).

A: Ask what the passenger wants.
B: Ask for a return ticket to Barcelona.
A: Ask when he/she wants to travel.
B: You want to go at 3 p.m. today.
A: Ask when he/she wants to come back.
B: Next week. Choose a date.
A: Ask if he/she wants 1st or 2nd class.
B: Decide.

Using a similar pattern, act out more role plays from the information below:

Passenger

Choose a destination:
   Bilbao   Salamanca
   Sevilla   Valencia

Decide departure date
Decide return date
Decide 1st or 2nd class

Ticket seller

You need to find out:
Destination
Single or return
When he/she wants to go
When he/she wants to come back
1st or 2nd class

A v

Look at the arrivals and departures board below. You will hear four announcements. Complete the information on the board by indicating the number of the platform as you hear it. If none is mentioned put a blank.

TREN	PROCEDENCIA	LLEGADA	DESTINO	SALIDA	VIA
TALGO	MADRID-CHAMARTIN	18 01	BARCELONA-TERMINO	18 09	
TALGO	BARCELONA-TERMINO	18 04	MADRID-CHAMARTIN	18 09	
AUTOMOTOR			TERUEL	18 30	3
TRANVIA			MORA la NUEVA	18 59	
ELECTROTREN	VIGO	19 24	BARCELONA-TERMINO	19 30	

A vi

Now listen to the announcements again and answer the following questions:

1. a) Where has this train come from?
   b) Where is it going?
   c) When will it leave?
2. a) What kind of train is it?
   b) When will it leave?
3. a) Where is this train going?
   b) The train is late. How late?
4. a) What kind of train is this?
   b) Where is it going?
   c) When will it arrive at the station?

A vii Speaking practice

Work in pairs. A asks for certain information, as in nos. 1–5 below. B finds the information from the information board which follows.

1. You want to go to Irún this afternoon. Ask if there is a train and what time it leaves.
2. You are meeting a friend off the train from Valencia. Ask what time it arrives.
3. There are two trains from Barcelona this afternoon. Ask what time they arrive and which one is the TALGO.
4. There are three trains to Barcelona this afternoon. Ask for details about each one.
5. You are meeting a friend off the train from La Coruña. Ask what time it arrives and if it is late.

LLEGADAS			LARGO RECORRIDO		SALIDAS
Tren	Procedencia	Llegada		Destino	Salida
TALGO	Madrid	15.05		Barcelona	15.15
Rápido	Valencia	15.25		Irún	15.35
TER	Bilbao	16.00		Barcelona	16.15
Semi-directo	S. Sebastián	16.30		Valencia	16.40
Electro-trén	Barcelona	17.30		Bilbao	17.40
TALGO	Barcelona	17.50		Madrid	18.00
Expreso	La Coruña	19.45		Barcelona	19.55

Oiga, por favor

vocabulary A

(La) RENFE	Spanish National Railway	Compruebe los datos	Check the details
Red Nacional de	Network	la hora de salida	departure time
Ferrocarriles Españoles		coche (m)	carriage
un billete para Madrid	a ticket for Madrid	destino	destination
un billete de ida	a single ticket	procedente de . . .	(arriving) from
un billete de ida y vuelta	a return ticket	retraso	delay
primera clase	first class		
primera clase	second class	*Types of trains:*	
segunda clase	What time does it leave?	TALGO	Spains fastest, most
¿A qué hora sale?	What time does it arrive?		comfortable train
Sale a las tres	It leaves at three	TER	A fast train, not as
Llega a las cinco	It arrives at five		luxurious as the TALGO
¿Cuándo quiere ir?	When do you want to go?	Electrotrén	A fast train
¿Cuándo quiere volver?	When do you want to return?	Rápido	Despite its name, this is a slow train which does long journeys
fumador	smoker	Expreso	Similar to a Rápido
no-fumador	non-smoker	Tranvía	
fecha (f)	date	Ferrobús	Short distance, local trains
viaje (m)	journey		
vía (f) andén (m)	platform		

B i** En el tren

You will hear 6 announcements which are made on the Talgo train between Barcelona and Madrid. Using options a–f below, decide at which stage of the journey each announcement is made.

a) Shortly before the meals are served
b) Announcing a film programme for later in the journey
c) Just before the film starts
d) As the train starts its journey
e) Just before arriving at a station
f) At various times throughout the journey, except when meals are being served in the restaurant car

B ii

You will hear 6 requests. For each one indicate the reason for the request.

Transporte público

B iii**

You will hear five people making suggestions or giving advice. Answer the following questions:

1 What is the meaning of 'día azul'?
2 Why is the passenger advised to make a reservation?
3 What are they thinking of doing while they wait for the train?
4 What time of day are they travelling? What do they want to do and why?
5 What has happened to this passenger? What must she do now?

B iv **Role play**

Act out the following short dialogues with a partner:

1 *Passenger:* Ask the guard if the bar is open at night.
  Guard: The bar will close at 10 p.m.

2 *Passenger:* Ask the guard what time lunch is served.
  Guard: They begin serving at 1 p.m.

  Passenger: Ask where the restaurant car is.
  Guard: It is towards the rear of the train.

3 *Passenger:* You have a ticket for today's 3 p.m. train to Granada. Ask if you can change it for tomorrow.
  Ticket seller: He/she can change the ticket but will have to go to a different part of the ticket office.

4 **

Passenger: Ask the left luggage officer how much it costs to leave your luggage for two hours.
Left-luggage officer: It costs 100 pts per hour per item. Warn him/her that the office closes in exactly two hours. Advise him/her to return promptly.

5 **

Passenger 1: On the train, you have reserved Seat no. 23 but you discover someone is already occupying the seat. Bring his/her attention to this and politely ask him/her to move.
Passenger 2: You have reserved the seat you are occupying. Show the other passenger your ticket and point out that he/she is in the wrong carriage.
Passenger 1: You discover that your reserved seat is in Carriage no. 18. This is no. 19.

6 **

Passenger: You plan to travel from Barcelona to Madrid (a distance of 600 kms). There are two trains you can take, a Talgo or a Rápido. Ask your friend which one you should take.
Friend: Explain to your friend the advantages of travelling by Talgo, (more comfortable, faster, good food etc) but that it is much more expensive than the Rápido. The Rápido stops at each station and takes a lot longer.
Passenger: Discuss the options and make your decision.

Oiga, por favor

vocabulary B

empleado	employee	reserva	reservation
viajero	traveller	reservar	to reserve
¡Feliz viaje!	Have a nice journey	Está reservado	It's reserved
próxima estación	the next station	revisor (*m*)	ticket inspector
servicios audiovisuales	audiovisual services	'Días azules'	'Blue days' (special days when tickets are cheaper)
auriculares (*m*)	headphones		
¡Bienvenidos!	Welcome		
señalizados	indicated	maleta	suitcase
señal	sign	consigna	left luggage
asiento	seat	taquilla	ticket office

C i En el autobús

You will hear 2 short dialogues. Answer the following questions:

1 How much does the ticket cost?

2 a) How much does a 'bonobús' cost?
   b) Where can you go with a 'bonobús'?
   c) How many journeys is it valid for?

vocabulary C

¿Para ir a . . .?	To get to . . .?	un bono-bús	a multi-journey bus ticket
la parada	stop		

Transporte público

D i En el aeropuerto

Rosa is going to catch an aeroplane. With a partner, discuss the things she should do before boarding the plane.

Now listen to the four short dialogues. For each one:

a) Decide where Rosa is.
b)** Say what she is being asked.

D ii**

Rosa is in the waiting area, waiting for her flight (to London) to be called. While she is there, there are a number of other flight announcements. For each flight number that you hear write down:

a) What the passengers have to do
b) Why

The flight numbers you will hear are:
BA 708   IB 602
IB 607   IB 709

Oiga, por favor

🎧 D iii**

You will hear three announcements that are given at different stages of a flight. Answer the following questions on each announcement:

1. **Airborne**
   a) What advice is given about seat belts?
   b) Where is it not permitted to smoke?
   c) How long will the flight last?
   d) What speed are they flying at?

2. **In flight**
   a) What will you be able to do in a few minutes?
   b) Where is the magazine which is mentioned in the announcement?

3. **Landing**
   a) What are you not permitted to do when you hear this announcement?
   b) What time is it in Barcelona?
   c) What is the weather like?
   d) What must you do if you are catching a connecting flight?

🎧 D iv**

You will hear an announcement on what to do in case of emergency. From the pictures opposite, select the three items you hear and indicate in which order you hear them.

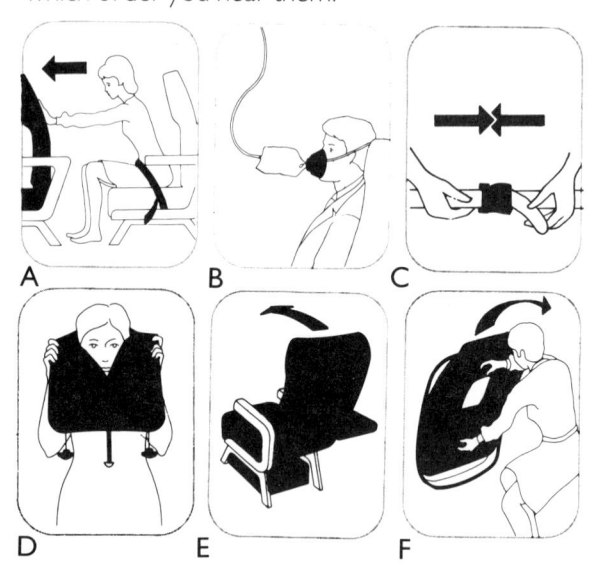

A   B   C

D   E   F

🎧 D v **En la aduana**

You will hear five questions from customs officers. Write down what they are asking in each case.

vocabulary D

facturación (f)	check-in
facturar	to check in
peso	weight
embarcar	to board
tarjeta de embarque	boarding pass
pasajero/a	passenger
vuelo	flight
volar	to fly
cinturón (m) de seguridad	safety belt
abrochar (se)	to fasten
desabrochar (se)	unfasten
impuestos	taxes
libre de impuestos	duty free
exceso	excess
equipaje (m)	luggage
detector (m)	detector
aviso	call
a bordo	on board
tripulación (f)	the crew
tomar tierra/aterrizar	to land
respaldo	the back of the seat
declarar	to declare
aeropuerto	airport
chaleco salvavidas	lifejacket
máscaras de oxígeno	oxygen masks
puertas y salidas de emergencia	emergency doors and exits
altitud (m)	altitude
velocidad (f)	speed
conexión (f)	connecting flight

En la ciudad y en la carreterra

A i Before you listen

Look at the picture. A woman is asking for information in a tourist office.

What is she asking? What other information can we get from a tourist office?

Practise questions in Spanish with your partner.

¿Podría darme un mapa de la provincia?

Sí, aquí tiene

A ii

1 Now listen to the dialogue in the tourist office and answer the following questions:

   a) What does the woman want?
   b) Where does she want to go?
   c) How is she going to travel?
   d) How far away is the place she wants to go to?

2 Now listen to the conversation again and choose the correct map from the three below. The tourist office is in Zaragoza.

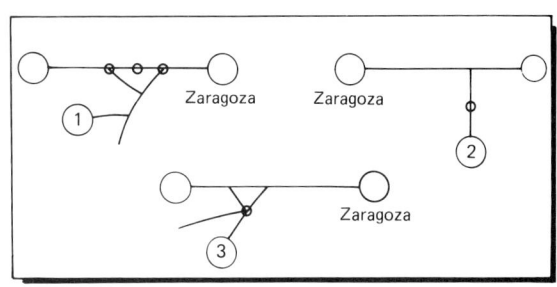

A iii

In each of the three dialogues 1–3 you will hear someone giving directions.

1 Which of the photos below corresponds to each dialogue and which is not relevant at all?

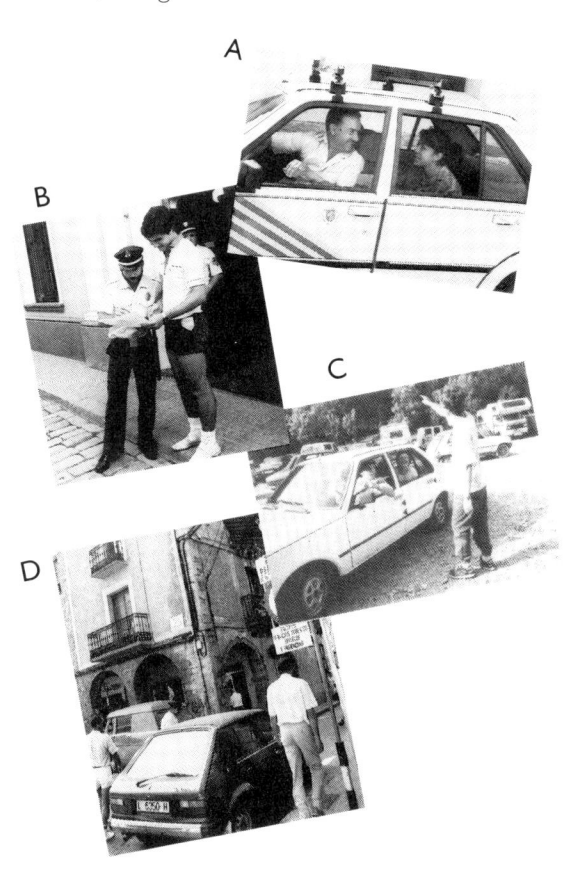

Oiga, por favor

2 Now look at the four maps below, listen again, and decide which map corresponds to each set of directions. Again there is an odd one out.

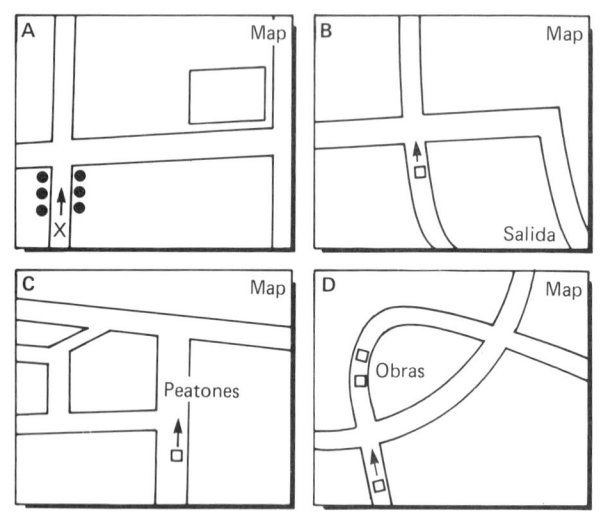

A	Map
B	Map (Salida)
C	Map (Peatones)
D	Map (Obras)

A iv En la ciudad

Look at the map of the centre of Zaragoza. Luis is in the Plaza de España and wishes to visit five monuments. Listen to the five dialogues in which he is given directions and find on the map the letter of the monument being talked about.

1 La Lonja
2 Torre de San Miguel
3 Torre de la Zuda
4 Murallas romanas
5 Puerta del Carmen

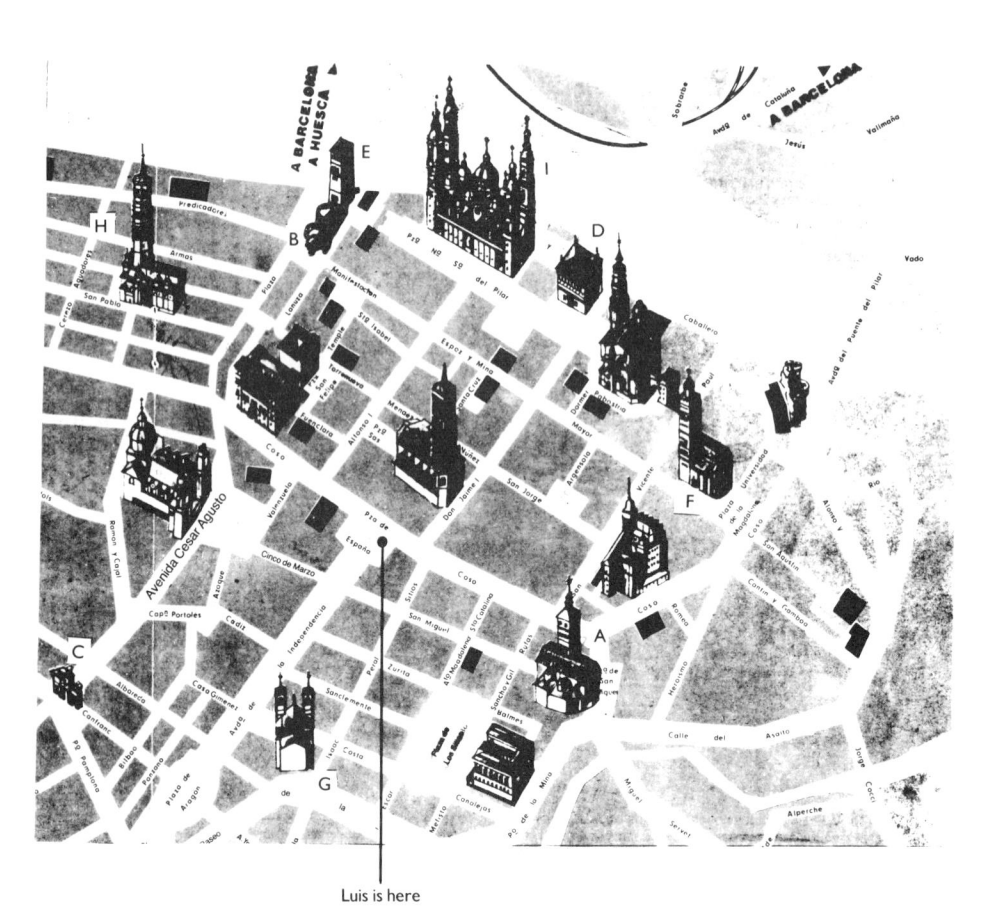

Luis is here

En la ciudad y en la carretera

A v Role play

Work in pairs. Take turns to ask how to get to the following places and follow your partner's instructions on the map. You are in the Plaza de España. Use the vocabulary list below.

1. La Magdalena (F)
2. Santa Engracia (G)
3. Iglesia de San Pablo (H)
4. Basílica del Pilar (I)

A vi Role play

In pairs, act out the following role plays which take place in the tourist office. In each, A is the tourist and B is the tourist officer.

1. A: Ask for a map of the town.
   B: Give him/her a map.
   A: Ask if the map has details of the main monuments.
   B: It has, but there is also a booklet with more information
   A: Ask for it.

2. A: You want some information about hotels in the town.
   B: Say there are some good hotels near the river and offer a brochure with a list of all the main hotels.
   A: Ask if they are very expensive.
   B: Say there are hotels of all prices. The details are in the brochure.

vocabulary A

¿Podría(s) darme . . . ?	Could you give me . . . ?
mapa (m) de la provincia	a map of the province
folleto	a brochure
plano de la ciudad	a plan of the city
monumento (m)	monument
excursión (f)	excursion/trip
¿Podría(s) decirme como ir a . . . ?	Could you tell me how to get to . . . ?
¿Para ir a . . . ?	To get to . . . ?
¿Dónde está(n) . . . ?	Where is/are . . . ?
salida	the way out
campo de fútbol	the football ground
aparcamiento	the car park
murallas	the ancient walls
iglesia	the church
torre (f)	the tower
río	the river
¿Por dónde puedo salir a la calle?	Which is the way out (to the street)?
avenida	the avenue
plaza	the square
puente (m)	the bridge
paseo	the main avenue
cruce (m)	the junction
¿Va/vas a pie?	Are you on foot?
Toma/Tome la primera calle a la derecha	Take the first street on the right
Cruza/Cruce la calle	Cross the road
a la izquierda	on the left
desvío	turning
lejos	a long way
cerca	near
al final de la calle	at the end of the street
enfrente de	opposite
al lado de	next to
Tuerza (torcer) a la izquierda	Turn to the left
Sigue/Siga recto	Carry straight on
Continúa/Continúe	Carry on
Sube/Suba	Go up
Baja/Baje	Go down
todo recto	straight on
hasta el final	to the end
semáforo	traffic lights
¿A cuántos kilómetros está?	How many kilometres is it?
¿A qué distancia está?	How far is it?
Está a 115 kilómetros	It's 115 kilometres away.
poner una multa	to fine someone
cortado por obras	(road) closed because of roadworks
guardia urbano (m)	traffic policeman

Oiga, por favor

B i Una visita a Belchite**

You will hear a guide showing some tourists around the old village of Belchite which was destroyed during the Spanish Civil War.

First she describes the story of Belchite. Answer the following questions:

1. How far is Belchite from Zaragoza?
2. Where was the new village built?
3. Why was the original village destroyed?
4. Did everyone leave the village after the war?
5. When was the new village finished?
6. How many people lived in Belchite before the war?
7. How is the new village different from the old?

B ii**

Now listen to the guide describing six different scenes in the village. Look at the photos below and match each description with the correct photo.

A

B

C

D

E

F

En la ciudad y en la carretera

C i En el coche

Listen to the following three short requests and match each one with the correct photo.

A B C

C ii

In this dialogue the woman is hiring a car. Decide whether the following statements are true or false:

1. She wants to hire a car for 10 days.
2. She wants it today.
3. The Renault costs 1,500 pts a day and 17 pts per kilometre.
4. The price includes insurance and petrol.
5. She has to pick up the car at 8 am.

C iii

Listen to the dialogue at a petrol station and answer the following questions:

1. What kind of petrol does the driver want?
2. How much does he want?
3. How much does it cost?
4. What other services does he require?

C iv**

Listen to the dialogue at a garage and decide which items in the list below are mentioned. Vocabulary list C will help you.

clutch   oil
brakes   accelerator
engine   seat belt
windscreen wipers

C v Role play

Work in pairs

1. Hiring a car (A = customer, B = hirer)

   A: You want to hire a car for three days.
   B: Ask how many people.
   A: Just you.
   B: Say you have a Renault 5 at a good price.
   A: You want something bigger for a long journey.
   B: Offer a *Seat 131*.
   A: Accept. Ask how much it costs.
   B: 2,300 ptas a day + 20 ptas a kilometre. This includes insurance.
   A: Say you will pick it up tomorrow morning.

vocabulary C

aquilar un coche	to hire a car	aire (m)	tyre pressure
seguro	insurance	neumáticos	tyres
carnet (m) de conducir	driving licence	motor (m)	engine
gasolina	petrol	los frenos	brakes
gasolinera	filling station	embrague (m)	clutch
súper	equivalent to 4-star	cinturón (m) de seguridad	seat belt
normal	equivalent to 2/3-star	Se ha soltado	It has come loose
lleno	full	aparcar	to park
¿Puede comprobar el aceite?	Could you check the oil?	arrancar	to start off (in a car)

Oiga, por favor

2 At the garage (A = customer, B = mechanic)

A: Say you want to bring your car in for a general service.

B: Ask if there is anything wrong with it.

A: Ask him/her to look at the brakes.

B: Say that the tyres may need replacing.

A: Agree. Ask him/her to change the windscreen wipers as well.

B: Agree.

A: Ask when you can bring it in.

B: He/She can leave it now if they want to.

A: Agree. Ask when it will be ready.

B: This afternoon.

D ¡ En camino

You will hear three dialogues (nos. 1–3) in which people are telephoning for help after a breakdown or accident. Copy the chart below.

Then, as you listen, choose the relevant details for each dialogue. Indicate your choice by putting the dialogue number in the correct place in each column.

Problem	Distance from Zaragoza	Car	Colour	Registration	Wait
a breakdown	30 kms	Ford Fiesta	blue	T-1392	30 mins
a puncture	105 kms	Renault 20	grey	Z-9811P	20 mins
accident	20 kms	Citroen	red	Z-4758N	15 mins
no petrol	45 kms	Seat 131	green	Z-6137S	60 mins

vocabulary D

¿Podrían enviar a alguien?	Could you send someone?	Me he quedado sin gasolina	I've run out of petrol.
pinchazo	puncture	lata	a tin
rueda de repuesto	spare wheel	grúa	breakdown truck
Seat (m)	Seat (a make of car)	avería	a breakdown
matrícula	registration number	autopista	motorway
¿Tardará mucho?	Will you be very long?		

E ¡**

You will hear part of a radio programme giving advice to drivers returning from their summer holidays in heavy traffic when there are a lot of accidents.

Before you listen, write down what you think the speaker will suggest under the following headings:

1 Checking the car before the journey.
2 On the journey.
3 A car carrying a family and luggage.
4 General advice for the return journey.

Compare your suggestions with a partner.

Now listen to the recording, compare your answers and note any others that you did not include.

El hotel y el apartamento

A i Before you listen

Look at the photograph. What does the woman want to know? What does the receptionist want to know? What other information do they want from each other?

Make up more questions in Spanish for a) the woman and b) the receptionist.

Speech bubbles in photo:
- ¿Tiene habitaciones libres?
- Sí. ¿Para cuántas noches?

A ii

Before you listen to the dialogue between the woman and the receptionist, look at the following list of statements. Then listen and decide whether each statement is true or false.

1 The woman wants two single rooms.
2 The hotel doesn't have any single rooms left.
3 The rooms have private bathrooms.
4 The woman and her family plan to stay for less than a week.
5 They want 'breakfast only' at the hotel.
6 Their rooms are next to each other.
7 They want a call in the morning.

A iii

In each of the two dialogues you will hear a client reserving a room by telephone. Copy the chart below and tick the correct boxes for each client. Two have already been done for you.

	First client	Second client
habitación individual		
habitación doble	✓	
pensión completa		
media pensión		
desayuno sólo		
con baño		✓
con ducha		
sin baño		
noches		

Oiga, por favor

A iv Role play

In pairs, take the part of C (the client) and R (the receptionist) in the following three situations. Use Vocabulary A to help you.

1. C: Ask for a double room with a bathroom.
   R: Ask how many nights they are going to stay.
   C: Three nights.
   R: Ask if they want full or half board.
   C: You want full board.

2. C: Ask for a single room with a shower.
   R: Ask how many nights they are going to stay.
   C: One week.
   R: Ask if they want full board.
   C: You want breakfast only.

3. C: Ask for two double rooms, both with bathroom.
   R: Ask how many nights they are going to stay.
   C: Four nights.
   R: Ask if they want full or half board.
   C: You want full board today and half board for the other three.

A v Role play**

Instructions as in Aiv.

1. C: Ask for two double rooms with a bathroom.
   R: Ask how many nights they want to stay.
   C: Three nights.
   R: You have a double room but it is only free for two nights. Offer a different room for the third night.
   C: Accept. Ask for full board.
   R: Your hotel only offers half board.
   C: Accept.

2. C: Ask for a single room with a shower.
   R: You only have a double room available.
   C: You don't think you can afford it.
   R: Say that they will pay less than the normal price of a double.
   C: Accept.
   R: Ask how many nights they want to stay.
   C: About a week but you aren't sure.
   R: Ask if they want full board.
   C: You only want breakfast.

   C: Ask for two double rooms with bathrooms.
   R: Ask how many nights they plan to stay.
   C: Four nights.
   R: You can only offer one double room and two singles for the first night. They can change the singles to a double on the second night.
   C: Accept.
   R: Ask if they want full board.
   C: You want half board.

En la ciudad y en la carretera

A vi

In this conversation the client is settling his bill. Listen and decide which of the two bills below is the correct one.

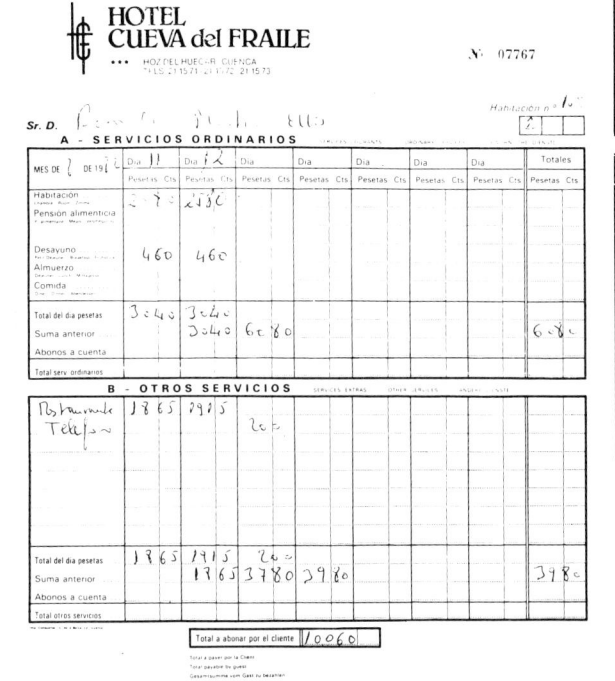

vocabulary A

¿Tiene habitaciones libres?	Have you any rooms free?
¿Tiene baño?	Has it got a bathroom?
ducha?	shower?
Quiero una habitación individual	I want a room single (room)
doble	double (room)
No me quedan individuales	I haven't any singles left
Me queda una.	I have *one* left
¿Para cuántas noches?	For how many nights?
pensión completa	full board
media pensión	half board
desayuno sólo	breakfast only
¿Me da(n) su documentación	Could you give me your documentation
El hotel está (casi) completo/lleno	The hotel is (almost) full
¿Puede llamarme/llamarnos a las siete?	Can you call me/us at seven?
¿Podría prepararnos la cuenta?	Could you prepare the bill for us?
dos cenas	two dinners
una llamada por teléfono	a telephone call

Oiga, por favor

B i

Copy the chart below

Listen to these six people complaining about problems in their hotel rooms.

1 Put the appropriate number next to each picture. The first is done for you.

2**Listen again and complete the rest of the chart. The first is done for you.

		Complaint	Solution
A			
B	1	The bulbs break frequently	She will replace it
C			
D			
E			
F			

Check your answers with a partner.

B ii Role play

In pairs, take the parts of the client (C) and the receptionist (R). Use the vocabulary B to help you.

1 C: Your room is very cold.
   R: Explain that the central heating has broken down.
   C: Ask for a heater (*una estufa*).
   R: Say you'll bring one in a moment.

2 C: Your room is noisy because of the traffic outside. Ask to change rooms.
   R: Say that there is no room free at the moment but that they can change tomorrow.

3 C: The people in the next room make a lot of noise when they come in late at night.
   R: Say you will speak to them.

4 C: Your window doesn't close properly.
   R: You will be up to fix it in a moment.

5 C: There are no towels in the bathroom.
   R: Say that someone will bring towels shortly.

**Now invent 5 more complaints and 5 responses.

vocabulary B

La luz (del baño) no funciona	The (bathroom) light doesn't work
El aire acondicionado no funciona	The air conditioning doesn't work
Hace calor en la habitación	The room is hot
La cama es incómoda	The bed is uncomfortable
La cama está rota	The bed is broken
El lavabo está muy sucio	The washbasin is very dirty
No hay toallas	There aren't any towels
No hay agua caliente en la ducha	There isn't any hot water in the shower
El agua está helada	The water is freezing cold
¿Podría arreglarlo/la/los/las?	Can you repair it/them?
Las bombillas se funden	The bulbs burn out
Se le ha olvidado a la chica (Ella) es muy despistada	The girl has forgotten She is very absent-minded
Hay que enchufar el calentador	You have to plug in the heater
Ahora (mismo) subo a poner otra	I'll come up and fit another one immediately
Ahora lo están arreglando	They're fixing it now.
Ahora subirá a limpiarla	She'll go up and clean it now
ventilador (*m*)	a fan
cambiarse a otra habitación	to move to another room

El hotel y el apartamento

C i**

Imagine you are working as a temporary receptionist in a Spanish hotel. Another receptionist is explaining the house rules to you. Make brief notes of these rules in English and then check your answers with a partner. The first is done for you.

1 Guests must be out of their rooms before 12 midday on the day they leave.

    2 Keys .....

    3 Breakfast .....

    4 No noise .....

    5 The hotel door .....

    6 Washing .....

    7 Animals .....

D i

Listen to the woman enquiring about renting a summer apartment and complete the missing information. Some details are done for you.

1 Types of apartment available:

    a) _____

    b) _____

    c) *two bedrooms furnished*

2 Three domestic appliances supplied:

    a) _____

    b) _____

    c) *cooker*

3 Where the apartments are:

    a) _____

    b) *outside the town*

4 Sports facilities offered:

    a) _____

    b) _____

5 Prices of one-bedroomed apartments:

    a) (15 days) _____

    b) (one month) _____

Oiga, por favor

D ii Role play

In pairs, take the part of the customer (C) and the agent (A). Use Vocabulary E to help you.

1. C: You want a one-room apartment for two weeks in July.
   A: You have some available.
   C: Ask how much they cost.
   A: Your prices range from 40,000 ptas to 60,000 ptas.
   C: You can't afford more than 45,000 ptas. Ask if they have one at that price.
   A: You have one for exactly 45,000 ptas.

2. C: Ask if the apartments are fully equipped.
   A: Your apartments have a fully equipped kitchen with cooker, fridge and washing machine.
   C: Ask about the bedroom.
   A: You supply blankets but not sheets.
   C: Ask if there are shops nearby.
   A: There is a shopping centre very near.

3**

The customer wants:

1 or 2 bedroom apt
Very near beach
15 June – 15 July

The agent has available:

2 bedroom apts
2 kms from beach
Complete calendar months only
Price: June – 100,000 ptas
      July – 130,000 ptas

4**

The customer wants:

2 bedroom flat
1 month (preferably August)
Cash limit: 100,000 ptas

The agent has available:

3 bedroom flats
July only
Price: 130,000 ptas
    (everything included)

vocabulary D

Queremos alquilar un apartamento	We want to rent an apartment	platos	plates
en la costa	on the coast	vasos	cups
un estudio	studio apartment	cubiertos	cutlery
de uno o dos dormitorios	with one or two bedrooms	ropa de cama	bedding
con cocina	with kitchen	Está(n) cerca del mar	It is (they are) near the sea
baño	bathroom	fuera del pueblo	outside the town
salón (*m*)	lounge	entre los pinos	amongst the pine trees
muebles (*m*)	furniture	jardín (*m*)	garden
Tiene...	It's got...	piscina	swimming pool
Está equipado de...	It's equipped with...	pista de tenis	tennis court
cocina	cooker/kitchen	todo incluído	everything included
lavadora (automática)	(automatic) washing machine	gas (*m*)	gas
frigorífico	refrigerator	electricidad (*f*)	electricity
		Ya lo pensaré	I'll think about it

En el camping y en la playa

A i Before you listen

In the picture, a camper is asking for information at a campsite.

¿Tiene sitio para una tienda?

Sí, ¿cuántos sois?

1 What does he want to know?
2 What question does the receptionist ask in reply?
3 What other information will the receptionist need?

Practise her questions in Spanish with a partner.

A ii

Now listen to the conversation between the camper and the receptionist and answer the following questions:

1 How long do they want to stay?
2 How many people want to camp?
3 What is the fee for the following per night?
   a) a tent   b) a person   c) a car
4 Is there a supermarket on the site?
5 Do the campers want mains electricity?

A iii

Look at the details for these three campsites:

A

Precio por noche	
👤	300 ptas
👧	(3–10 años) 200 ptas
🚶	—
🚗	300 ptas
🛵	250 ptas
⛺	300 ptas
▲	250 ptas

B

Precio por noche	
👤	300 ptas
👧	200 ptas
🚶	(0–3) 150 ptas
🚗	300 ptas
🛵	280 ptas
⛺	300 ptas
▲	250 ptas

C

Precio por noche	
👤	300 ptas
👧	250 ptas
🚗	280 ptas
🛵	250 ptas
⛺ ▲	300 ptas
🚐	300 ptas

Now listen to two people, each booking into a campsite (Dialogues 1 and 2). Decide which campsite (A, B or C) each camper is booking into.

Oiga, por favor

A iv

Now listen to the dialogues again and follow the instructions for each.

Dialogue 1: Indicate whether the following statements are *True* or *False*.

1 They want to stay about two weeks.
2 The receptionist will keep their identity cards for the first day of their stay and will then return them.

Dialogue 2: Answer the following questions.

1 How many people are there?
2 What did they bring with them?
3 Does the child have to pay?
4 What does the receptionist ask for?

A v Role play

Now practise similar dialogues (1–4 below) with a partner.

1 *Receptionist:* Greet the campers.
  Camper: Ask if there are spaces available for a two-person tent.
  Receptionist: There are spaces. How many nights?
  Camper: The weekend, two nights.
  Receptionist: What kind of vehicle?
  Camper: A small motorcycle. Ask how much it will all cost.
  Receptionist: Choose the details from the price lists above.

2 *Receptionist:* Greet the camper.
  Camper: Ask if there are spaces.
  Receptionist: Ask how many people and for how many nights.
  Camper: A family of five, a couple and three children, one of whom is under 3. For six nights.
  Receptionist: There is space near the beach but a long way from the shop and the showers.
  Camper: That's fine. Ask about prices.
  Receptionist: Choose from the lists above.

3** One of you must take the part of the camper and the other the part of the receptionist. Choose which of the sites above you wish to camp on and make up a dialogue.

4** Do the same again, but this time, if you are the receptionist, invent one or two problems for the campers. Here are some suggestions:
  a) no space in the shade
  b) available for fewer nights than requested
  c) no mains electricity
  d) near the railway

vocabulary A

¿Tiene(s) sitio para una tienda?	Have you space for a tent?
para el fin de semana	for the weekend
para dos noches	for two nights
¿Quedan sitios cerca de la playa?	Is there any space near the beach?
piscina	swimming pool
Está lleno	It's full
¿Cuántos sois/son?	How many of you are there?
Somos tres	There are three of us
¿Cuántas noches piensan quedarse?	How many nights do you intend to stay?
¿Cuánto tiempo van a quedarse?	How long are you going to stay?
un matrimonio y un niño	a married couple and a child
conectar	to connect
electricidad (f)	electricity
electricista (m)	electrician
folleto	brochure
documentación (f)	documentation
vehículo	vehicle
moto (f)	motorcycle
caravana	caravan
lancha	small boat
IVA incluido	VAT included

El hotel y el apartamento

B i

You will hear an interview with Montse, whose parents run a campsite. Look at the statements below and indicate whether they are *True* or *False*.

1 The campsite opened about twenty years ago.
2 Most of the campers on the site are foreigners.
3 The site is near the beach.
4 You have to pay extra for hot showers.
5 Cars cannot enter the site after midnight.

B ii

In the interview (Bi) Montse tells Rosa about the facilities at the campsite. Look at the symbols below and with a partner or your teacher, decide what they represent in Spanish.

Now listen to the interview again and indicate the order in which each facility is mentioned.

B iii Role play

In pairs, take the parts of the receptionist and a camper. If you are the camper, you must find out if the campsite has the following facilities and, if so, the opening times. The receptionist must find the information in the brochure below to answer the questions.

The camper wants to know about:
   public telephones
   post office
   shop
   bar
   restaurant
   currency exchange

For example:
Campista: Por favor, ¿hay servicio de lavandería?
Recepcionista: Sí, hay.
Campista: ¿A qué hora está abierta?
Recepcionista: De nueve a seis de la tarde.

Oiga, por favor

B iv

You will hear two friends comparing 'Camping l 'Alba' and 'Camping Gavina'. Look at the pictures below and, from the information in the conversation, match three pictures with each campsite.

1

2

3

4

5

6

L'Alba: Nos_____   _____   _____

Gavina: Nos_____   _____   _____

B v 🎧

Listen to the same conversation again and write the appropriate letter ('A' for l'Alba and 'G' for Gavina) for each of the following statements.

1. Es más barato.
2. Está más cerca de la playa.
3. Tiene restaurante.
4. Tiene más árboles.
5. La piscina es mejor.
6. Hay más espacio entre las tiendas.
7. Hay más familias con niños pequeños.
8. Hay campo de fútbol.
9. Hay mucho polvo.
10. Está cerca de la vía del tren.

B vi Speaking practice

In Spanish, discuss with your partner which of the two campsites you prefer. Give your reasons, using the information above to help you.

B vii 🎧

You will hear a number of campsite announcements. Look at the times below and match each announcement with the time mentioned. Then listen again and complete the blanks with the appropriate activity or service. The first is done for you.

5–6 p.m. Doctor's surgery

11 a.m. tomorrow _____

From 8 p.m. _____

11.30 p.m. _____

at 8 p.m. _____

B viii Role play**

In the following role plays, a camper is asking the receptionist for information. In pairs, take the parts of the camper, whose questions are listed below, and the receptionist, who should refer to the site regulations to give the information requested.

The camper's questions:
1. You are going out this evening. Will you be able to bring the car back on to the site at about midnight.
2. You want to know if two friends aged 15 years can camp on the site without their parents.
3. You want to know what time reception closes.
4. Can you bring your dog on your camping holiday?
5. Can you build a real fire to do your cooking?

Reglamento del Camping Alba

- La entrada de Recepción queda cerrada desde las 21h hasta las 8h.

  El camping no se hace responsable de sus pertenencias.

- Al camping pueden entrar todos los campistas mayores de 16 años y todos los menores de esta edad si van acompañados de sus padres o personas mayores responsables de sus actos.

- Se respetará el silencio en todo el camping desde las 24h hasta las 7 de la mañana.

- No se permitirá la entrada de vehículos a aquellos campistas que regresen o lleguen al campamento después de las 24 horas. Para estos casos se dispone de amplio parking a la entrada del camping donde deberán permanecer los vehículos hasta las 7 de la mañana.

- Se permite la entrada al camping a los perros siempre que los mismos permanezcan atados junto a sus dueños y no molesten a los vecinos.

- Queda prohibido hacer fuego de leña o de otro tipo que no sea originado por bombonas de gas butano o propano.

Oiga, por favor

vocabulary B

Se abrió hace veinte años	It opened twenty years ago	aparcamiento	car park
una zona tranquila	a peaceful area	caja fuerte	a safe
arenas finas (f)	fine sand	campista (m/f)	camper
agua limpísima (f)	very clean water	tranquilidad (f)	peace
holandeses	Dutch people	seguridad (f)	safety, security
alemanes	German people	guarda (m/f)	guard
italianos	Italian people	vigilar	to supervise
turismo nacional	national tourism	deportes (m)	sports
a cien metros de la playa	a hundred metres from the beach	gas butano (m)	butane gas
		lavado de coches (m)	car wash
árbol (m)	tree	Se admiten animales	Animals admitted
juegos infantiles (m)	children's games	sombra	the shade
cable (m)	electrical cable	hierba	grass
enchufe (m)	plug (electrical)	ambiente (m)	atmosphere
agua caliente (f)	hot water	polvo (del camino)	dust (from the road)
gratis	free	visitante (m/f)	visitor
lavandería	laundrette	Se ruega . . .	Please . . .
servicio médico	medical service	recinto	area
ATS (asistente técnico sanitário)	nurse	campeonato de natación	swimming championships
		inscribirse	to register
medicamento	medicine		

C i

Manolo went for a walk on the beach where he met several people and did a number of interesting things. You will hear 5 short dialogues (1–5). Match each dialogue with the correct picture below.

A

B

C

50

En el camping y en la playa

C ii

Now write the appropriate captions to accompany each picture.
For example:
Picture A – Manolo comprando un helado.

C iii

Now listen to dialogues Ci again and answer the following questions:

¿Cuánto cuesta . . .

– un polo de naranja? _____

– un toldo? _____

– un cursillo de windsurf? _____

– una entrada para la discoteca? _____

– una hamaca? _____

¿Cuánto tiempo . . .

– dura un cursillo de windsurf? _____

– quiere Manolo tener la hamaca y el toldo?
_____

– van a estar Juan y sus amigos pescando atún?
_____

vocabulary C

un toldo	sunshade	un helado de bombón	a chocolate ice cream
una hamaca	deckchair	un crocanti	an ice cream with chocolate and nuts
pescar	to fish		
atún (*m*)	tuna	un polo	ice lolly
¿Cuánto rato vais a estar?	How long are you going to be?	muy rico	very tasty
		la verbena	a type of party
un par de horas	a couple of hours	gratis	free
¡Oiga!	Excuse me (*Lit:* Hear)	cursillo	short course

51

De compras

A i Before you listen

Look at the picture of a shopper buying fruit and vegetables.

Póngame un kilo de plátanos, por favor.

¿Qué le pongo?

1 What is the shop assistant saying?
2 What kind of fruit does the shopper want to buy?
3 What other fruit or vegetables might she ask for?

Practise in Spanish with a partner.

A ii

Copy the chart below.

1 In the left hand column you will see a list of different kinds of fruit and vegetables. Listen to the conversation and tick off the items the shopper buys.
2 Now listen again and write down the quantity and price of each item in columns 2 and 3.
     One item is done for you.

Item	Quantity	Price
apples		
bananas	1 kg	150 pts
strawberries		
grapes		
pears		
oranges		
potatoes		
carrots		
lettuce		
tomatoes		
melon		

A iii Speaking practice

Look at the pictures of the various kinds of shop or stall in a typical Spanish shopping centre.

De compras

Using Vocabulary A to help you, make a shopping list of about 6 or 7 items and then practise asking for them in Spanish with a partner.

vocabulary A

La frutería/la verdulería	fruiterer's/greengrocer's
un kilo de . . .	a kilo of . . .
medio kilo de . . .	half a kilo of . . .
un cuarto de . . .	a quarter of . . .
plátanos (m)	bananas
naranjas (f)	oranges
manzanas (f)	apples
patatas (f)	potatoes
uva (f)	grapes
carnicería	the butcher's
carne (f)	meat
chuletas (f) de cordero	lamb chops
gordas	thick ones
finas	thin ones
salchichas (f)	sausages
de varias clases	of various kinds
¿Cuál le pongo?	Which one shall I serve you?
pescadería	the fishmonger's
pescado	fish
sardinas	sardines
merluza	hake
trucha	trout
gambas	prawns
a rodajas	in slices
a filetes	filleted
la tienda de comestibles	the grocer's
jamón serrano (m)	smoked ham
jamón york (m)	cooked ham
cien gramos de chorizo	a hundred grams of spicy hard sausage
una lata de olivas	a tin of olives
media docena de huevos	half a dozen eggs
un litro de aceite	a litre of oil
la panadería	the baker's
una barra de pan	a loaf of bread
panecillos (m)	rolls
la pastelería	the cake shop
un pastel	a cake
¿Qué desea?	What would you like?
¿Qué le pongo?	What can I get you?
¿Le sirven?	Is anyone serving you?
Póngame/Deme . . .	Give me . . .
¿Qué precio tiene/n . . .?	How much is/are . . . ?
Están/Son a 60 pesetas el kilo	They are 60 pesetas a kilo
¿Algo más?/¿Alguna cosa más?	Anything else?

Oiga, por favor

A iv

The person who wrote the shopping list below forgot to include a number of items. Listen to the four dialogues, each in a different shop, and make your own list of the missing items. Compare your answers with those of a partner.

```
Carnicería
4 chuletas (cordero)
pescadería
sardinas (2 kgs)
¼ gambas
merluza (1 kg)

Comestibles
chorizo    (100 grs)
olivas     (lata)
aceite     (1 litro)
huevos     (6)
panadería / pastelería
pan (2 barras)
panecillos (3)
```

A v Role play

Work in pairs. In turns, take the parts of the shopper and the assistant. Use Vocabulary A to help you. If you are the assistant, make a note of the prices as the shopper buys.

1 La frutería/la verdulería

   Assistant: Ask who is next.
   Shopper: It's your turn. Ask how much the pears cost.
   Assistant: ____ pts a kilo.
   Shopper: You want a kilo. Now ask for half a kilo of grapes.
   Assistant: Green or black grapes?
   Shopper: Decide. Now ask for 2 kilos of oranges.
   Assistant: Which ones? ____ pts a kilo or ____ pts a kilo?
   Shopper: Decide.
   Assistant: Anything else?
   Shopper: Decide. Continue if you wish.
   Assistant: When the shopper has finished buying work out the total cost.

2 La carnicería

   Assistant: Ask who is next.
   Shopper: It's your turn.
   Assistant: Ask what you can get him/her.
   Shopper: Ask the price of the pork chops.
   Assistant: ____ pts a kilo.
   Shopper: Ask for four big chops and ask the assistant to cut off the fat (*quitar la grasa*).
   Assistant: Anything else?
   Shopper: A leg of lamb for roasting.
   Assistant: Large or small?
   Shopper: For four persons, large.
   Assistant: Anything else?
   Shopper: You decide.
   Assistant: When the shopper has finished buying, work out the total cost.

3 Make up more role plays like the above, and also with variations to practise your speaking. Other shops are: la pescadería, la tienda de comestibles, la panadería.

B i

You will hear five short dialogues. Each one takes place in one of the shops shown at the top of page 55. Match each dialogue to one of the shops and give the names of the shops.

B ii **

Now listen to the dialogues again and answer the following questions:

1 What other item does she buy apart from the eau de cologne?
2 Why are there two prices on the eau de cologne?
3 Does he buy anything besides newspapers?
4 Why does she want to buy a fan?
5 What does the assistant offer her?
6 How many things does the shopper buy for 85 pesetas? What are they?
7 What is wrong with the files?
8 Why does she buy them?

De compras

B iii Role play**

Act out the following role plays with a partner.

1

Customer

You want to buy some toothpaste but your normal brand is not there. Ask about it. The assistant will offer you another one. You aren't sure. Make a decision.

Assistant   You have sold out of the customer's normal toothpaste. Offer a different one which is on special offer (3 for the price of 2).

2

Customer

You want to buy some perfume. The assistant shows you the best perfume in the shop. It's too expensive. Ask to see something cheaper and take the advice of the assistant on which one to buy.

Assistant   The customer wants a bottle of perfume. Show him/her the best you have. If he/she turns it down show a selection and recommend one.

3   Now act out similar role plays in each of the following shops: la joyería, la librería, el estanco. Use Vocabulary B to help you.

vocabulary B

perfumería/la droguería	chemist's	sello	stamp
bronceador (*m*)	suntan oil	caja de cerillas	box of matches
pastilla de jabón	bar of soap	librería/la papelería	stationer's
frasco de colonia	bottle of eau de cologne	carpeta	file
quiosco	kiosk	diccionario	dictionary
periódico	newspaper	tamaño (*m*)	size
revista	magazine	defecto	defect
joyería	jeweller's		
tienda de regalos	gift shop	Se lo voy a mostrar	I'll show it to you
regalo	gift	Está muy bien de precio	It's a good price
abanico	fan	Está de oferta	It's on offer
pendientes (*m*)	earrings	Me lo llevo	I'll take it
algo sencillo	something simple	Me lo quedo	I'll take it
		Me quedo con esto	I'll take this one
estanco	shop that sells tobacco, stamps, envelopes	Está rebajado/a	It's reduced
		Le puedo hacer un descuento	I can give you a discount
postal (*f*)	postcard		
sobre (*m*)	envelope		

Oiga, por favor

C i

Javier is in a department store buying a shirt. Listen to the conversation between him and the sales assistant and answer the following questions:

1. What colour does he want?
2. Does the assistant have the shirt he wants?
3. What can you say about the cost of the shirt?
4. What size does he take?
5. How is he going to pay?

C ii

In the two dialogues you will hear people buying items of clothing. Copy the chart below and complete it by ticking the appropriate boxes in each column.

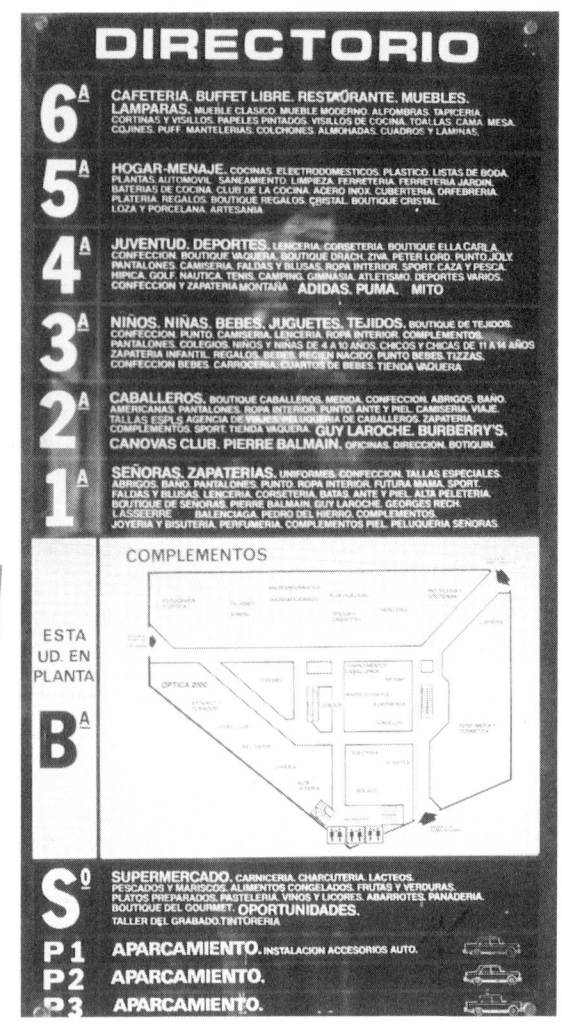

	Article		Colour		Size		Price	
1	trousers	☐	red	☐	40	☐	5000 pts	☐
	dress	☐	yellow	☐	42	☐	5500 pts	☐
	coat	☐	blue	☐	44	☐	6000 pts	☐
2	shirt	☐	white	☐	39	☐	4000 pts	☐
	cardigan	☐	green	☐	40	☐	4500 pts	☐
	jersey	☐	black	☐	42	☐	4750 pts	☐

De compras

C iii**

You will hear a number of announcements advertising bargains to be found in FAY, a large department store. Copy and complete the chart below. The first item is done for you.

Artículo	Planta	Departamento	Precio
vestido	segunda	ropa señora	3500 pts
pantalones	_____	_____	_____
_____	_____	_____	6000 pts
_____	cuarta	_____	_____
_____	_____	_____	875 pts
_____	_____	baterías de cocina	_____

1** Why are there reductions in FAY?
2** What time of the year is it?

C iv**

In the following six short dialogues, each of the customers is asking to change something they bought recently. Copy and complete the table of information below. Some items are already done for you.

**

Now listen again to the two dialogues where the customer was unable to change the article. Write down the reason in each case.

	Article	Reason for change?	Can he/she change it?
1	shirt		Yes
2		a scratch	
3			No
4		a hole	
5	dictionary		
6			Yes

Oiga, por favor

C v Role play**

With a partner, act out role plays on the following pattern.

The customer
Choose articles from the list below. Take it back to the shop where you bought it. State your reasons for wanting to change it.

The assistant
Find out when the customer bought the article. Find out why he/she wants to change it. Ask to see the receipt. Decide whether he/she can change it. (If there are any instructions, check that they have been followed.)

a radio/doesn't work
a jacket/you don't like the colour OR it's too small
an alarm clock/the alarm doesn't work properly
a set of wine glasses/one was broken in the box

Think of further examples.

C vi

In the first dialogue of Civ the assistant changed a shirt which the customer had returned. Listen to a continuation of that conversation as the assistant explains the washing and ironing instructions carefully to the customer. Indicate which of the three labels below belongs to the article.

A

Estos calcetines están fabricados con las mejores materias.

ALGODON 100 %

D.N.I. 38.650.810 - Fte.-B 675.
Calella   Spain

B

victoria

Este modelo lleva los colorantes de mayor calidad y para su mejor resultado, recomendamos.

• LAVAR EN AGUA FRIA ó COMO MAXIMO A 20º C.
• NO DEJAR EN REMOJO.
• UTILIZAR DETERGENTE NEUTRO.

Muchas gracias por su confianza
VICTORIA

C

LAVADO

No superar los 45° C de temperatura

Utilizar jabon neutro

No usar lejia

Planchar a menos de 110°C

No centrifugar

De compras

vocabulary C

caro/a	expensive
barato/a	cheap
camisa (de manga corta)	a (short-sleeved) shirt
blusa (de algodón)	a (cotton) blouse
vestido amarillo	a yellow dress
verde/azul/negro	green/blue/black
estampado	patterned
jersey (m)	a sweater
chaqueta	a jacket/a cardigan
No me queda	I don't have any left
Tengo un modelo parecido	I have a similar model
probar	to try on
¿Puedo probármelo/la/los/las?	Can I try it/them on?
¿Puedo cambiarlo/la/los/las?	Can I change it/them?
talla	size
¿Cómo le/te va/van?	How does it/do they fit you?
Me va/van bien	It/they fit(s)/suit(s) me well.
pagar en efectivo	pay in cash
pagar con tarjeta	pay by credit card
reformas (f)	building alterations
artículos	the articles
boutique (f)	boutique
planta segunda/tercera	second/third floor
planta baja	ground floor
sótano	basement
ropa (de última moda)	clothes (in the latest fashion)
hecho/a a mano	made by hand
ropa de señora	women's clothes
ropa de caballero	men's clothes
sección (f)	section
departamento	department
silla plegable	folding chair
mesa	table
bolso nevera	ice bag
espejo	mirror
baterías de cocina	saucepan set
cazo	saucepan
acero inoxidable	stainless steel
Pedimos disculpas por las molestias	We apologise for any inconvenience
seguir las instrucciones de lavado	to follow the washing instructions
ticket (m)/recibo	receipt
disco	a record
rayado	scratched
zapatos	shoes
agujero	a hole
unas hojas	some pages
Faltan unas hojas	There are some pages missing
Huele mal	It smells bad
lavar en la lavadora	to wash in the washing machine
lavar a mano	to wash by hand
la etiqueta	label
planchar	to iron
una prenda muy delicada	a very delicate item of clothing

D i

You will hear five radio advertisements. Match four of the five you hear with four of the illustrations below and on page 60.

Oiga, por favor

LA CALIDAD NUESTRA RAZÓN DE SER.
LECHE PASCUAL UPERISADA

Nuestra razón de ser es ofrecer constantemente a todos los consumidores la más alta calidad.

Utilizamos la más avanzada tecnología en la uperisación y el envasado en Brik, garantizando al consumidor la excelente calidad de Leche PASCUAL, única en sabor y rica en propiedades nutritivas.

Aquí tiene las lavadoras más prácticas del mercado.

Las lavadoras Lynx. Fuertes y duraderas. Lavadoras con lavado en frío, programa económico, dispositivo antiarrugas y programas para lana. Lynx las lavadoras más prácticas, duras y duraderas del mercado.

Electrodomésticos **Lynx**
Duros que duran.

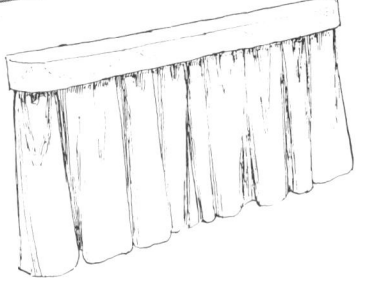

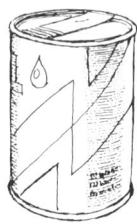

Elosúa. El sabor en su punto.

ELOSUA
GARANTIA DE CALIDAD

MUEBLES AUXILIARES PARA EL HOGAR
* Mesas
* Sillas
* Escaleras
* Cunas
* Mesas T.V.
* Tablas de planchar

en MADERA y METÁLICOS

Ruiz, S.C.
Camino Vilella, 10 - ALCIRA (Valencia)

Calzados AUDAZ
MANISES   VALENCIA

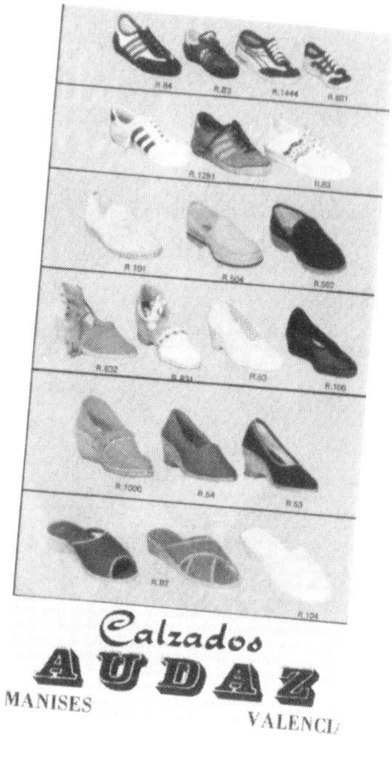

D ii**

Now invent an advertisement for any of the above products *not* mentioned on the tape.

En el banco y en correos

A i Before you listen

Look at the picture. What does the woman want to know? What does the bank employee ask to see?

¿Se pueden cobrar estos cheques de viaje aquí?

Sí. ¿Me deja su pasaporte?

A ii

Look at the pictures below. As you listen to the dialogue, put the pictures in the right order.

A

B

C

D

Oiga, por favor

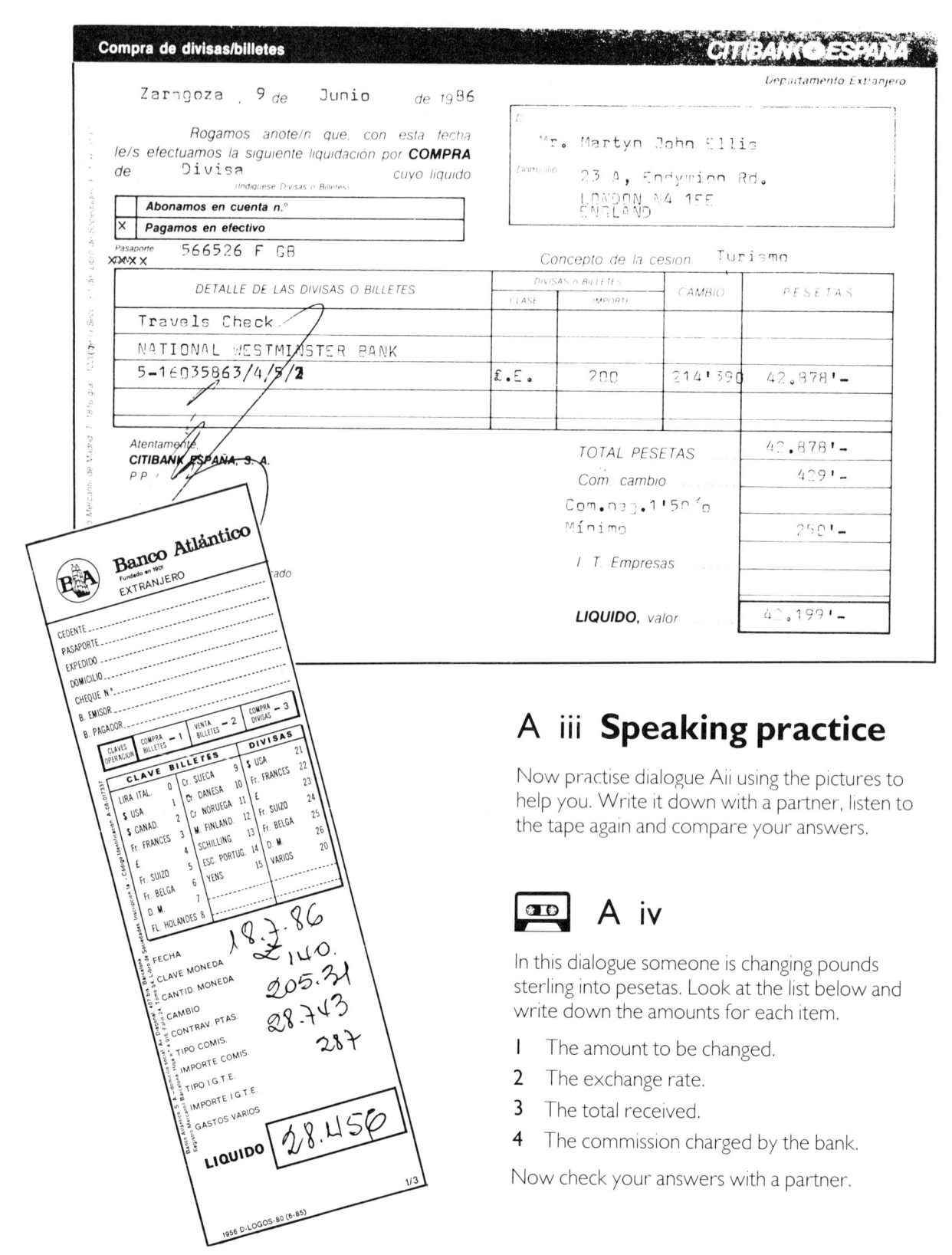

A iii Speaking practice

Now practise dialogue Aii using the pictures to help you. Write it down with a partner, listen to the tape again and compare your answers.

A iv

In this dialogue someone is changing pounds sterling into pesetas. Look at the list below and write down the amounts for each item.

1 The amount to be changed.
2 The exchange rate.
3 The total received.
4 The commission charged by the bank.

Now check your answers with a partner.

En el banco y en Correos

A v **Role play****

Now look at the document below. It is similar to the one being discussed in dialogue Aiv. Act out the parts of the customer and the bank employee using the information on the document, and using the original dialogue to help you.

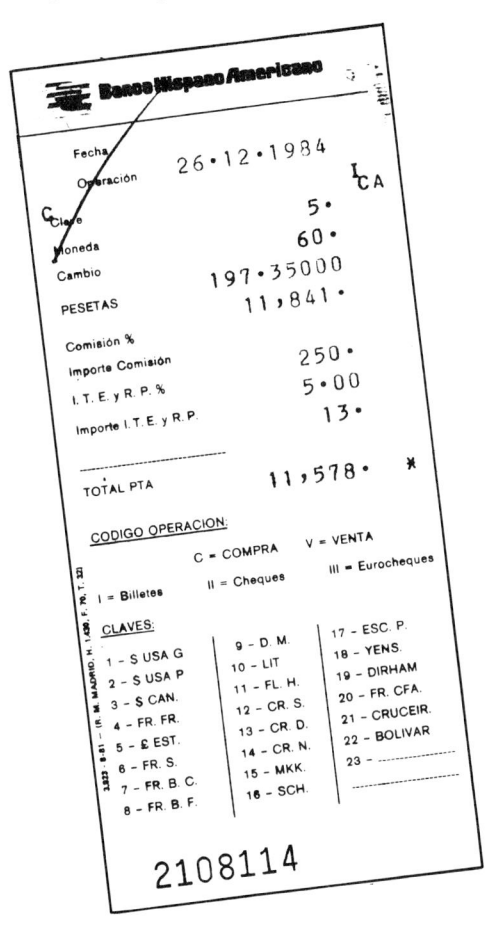

```
Banco Hispano Americano
Fecha           26.12.1984
Operación                    C A
Clave                      5.
Moneda                    60.
Cambio             197.35000
PESETAS             11,841.
Comisión %
Importe Comisión         250.
I.T.E. y R.P. %         5.00
Importe I.T.E. y R.P.     13.

TOTAL PTA           11,578.  *

CODIGO OPERACION:
            C = COMPRA   V = VENTA
            II = Cheques  III = Eurocheques
         I = Billetes
CLAVES:
1 - S USA G    9 - D.M.     17 - ESC. P.
2 - S USA P   10 - LIT      18 - YENS
3 - S CAN.    11 - FL. H.   19 - DIRHAM
4 - FR. FR.   12 - CR. S.   20 - FR. CFA.
5 - £ EST.    13 - CR. D.   21 - CRUCEIR.
6 - FR. S.    14 - CR. N.   22 - BOLIVAR
7 - FR. B. C. 15 - MKK      23 - ........
8 - FR. B. F. 16 - SCH.

                2108114
```

A vi **Role play**

Below is a conversation between a customer who wants to cash traveller's cheques and a bank employee. Act out the role play with a partner.

BE: Greet the customer.
C: Ask if you can change traveller's cheques here.
BE: You can. How much do you want to change?
C: £100 (sterling).
BE: Ask for the customer's passport. Then ask him/her to sign the cheque.?
C: Ask where you have to sign.
BE: Indicate the spot.
C: Ask what the exchange rate is.
BE: 219 pesetas to the pound.

vocabulary A

¿Dónde puedo cobrar estos cheques? (de viaje)	Where can I cash these (traveller's) cheques?	comisión (f)	commission
¿Se pueden cambiar estos billetes?	Is it possible to change these notes?	¿Me deja su pasaporte?	Could you give me your passport?
libras esterlinas (f)	pounds sterling	cambio (m)	change
Vaya a caja	Go to the cash till	¿Puede rellenar este papel?	Could you fill in this paper?
ventanilla de pagos	the window for withdrawing cash	(Se pueden cambiar) si las firmas son conformes	(You can change them) if the signatures are in order
¿Me lo firma (Vd)?	Could you sign it?		

Oiga, por favor

🎧 B i

You will hear 8 short dialogues which take place in a bank. Rearrange the list below in the order in which you hear the items. The first one is done for you.

a) Sending money abroad
b) Opening a foreign resident's account
c) Withdrawing cash from an account
d) Opening a savings account   [1]
e) Asking to speak to the manager
f) Cashing foreign bank notes
g) Reporting stolen traveller's cheques
h) Paying in cash to an account

Check the order with your partner and then with your teacher.

🎧 B ii**

Now listen again. This time write down one thing the customer needs to produce or do in each case.

Check your answers with your partner. The first item is done for you.

1 Opening a savings account.
    You need your identity card.

---

vocabulary B

Quiero...	I want (I'd like) to...	los detalles de la cuenta	details of the account
abrir una cuenta corriente	open a current account	su libreta	your passbook
abrir una cuenta de ahorro	open a savings account	¿Qué tengo que hacer?	What do I have to do?
mandar/enviar dinero al extranjero	send money abroad	Tiene que...	You have to (You'll have to)...
ingresar dinero	pay in some money	Hay que...	It'll be necessary to...
sacar dinero	withdraw some money	rellenar este papel	fill in this paper
		esperar	wait
¿Es extranjero/a?	Are you a foreigner?	hacer una visita más tarde	make an appointment for later
¿Tiene...	Have you got (Do you have)...		
permiso de residencia	a residence permit		
los números de los cheques	the cheque numbers		

En el banco y en Correos

C i

In this dialogue Rosa is asking Javier to post a letter. As you listen, answer the questions below:

1. Rosa asks Javier to post a letter. Where does she want him to post it?
2. What does Javier suggest?
3. Why is this not possible?
4. What has Rosa forgotten to put on the letter?
5. Write it down.

Códigos postales

Oiga, por favor

C ii**

Listen to the dialogue. Javier is in the post office talking to the post office employee.
Mention three things he has to do.

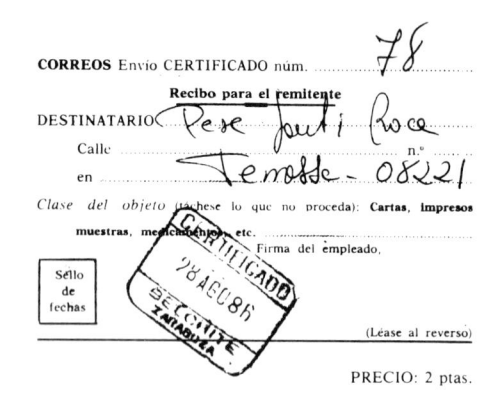

1 _____
2 _____
3 _____

CORREOS Envío CERTIFICADO núm. _78_
Recibo para el remitente
DESTINATARIO _Pere Jauti Roce_
Calle _____ n.º ___
en _Temosse - 08221_
Clase del objeto (táchese lo que no proceda): **Cartas, impresos muestras, medicamentos,** etc.
Firma del empleado.
Sello de fechas
(Léase al reverso)
PRECIO: 2 ptas.

C iii

You will hear 5 short dialogues in a post office. Rearrange the list below in the order in which you hear the items.

a) Sending a parcel
b) Sending a giro
c) Collecting a parcel
d) Buying stamps
e) Sending an airmail letter

C iv Role plays

Act out, with a partner, the following role plays. In each case, C is the customer and PE is the post office employee.

1 C: You want to send a parcel to England.
   PE: Ask if they want to send it airmail.
   C: Say yes and ask how much it will cost.
   PE: Give the necessary information.
   C: Say that's fine.

2 C: You want to send a telegram to England. Ask how much it costs per word.
   PE: Give the information.
   C: Ask what you have to do.
   PE: Give the customer the form.

3 C: Ask for three stamps for England and five for Spain.
   PE: Give them.
   C: Ask how much.
   PE: Say how much.

4 PE: You call at the customer's door with a recorded delivery parcel.
   C: The parcel is for your friend, who isn't here. Offer to sign.
   PE: Say that's fine.

vocabulary C

¿Vas a salir?	Are you going out?
¿Podrías echar esta carta?	Could you post this letter?
un buzón	post box
Quiero mandar un giro (postal)	I want to send a giro
una carta por avión	airmail letter
una carta certificada	recorded delivery letter
Quiero recoger un paquete	I want to collect a parcel
Te has olvidado de poner	You have forgotten to put
el código postal	the post code
Rellene (Vd) este papel	Fill in this paper
impreso	form
formulario	form
Ponga (Vd) estos sellos	Put these stamps on
la ventanilla de certificados	the recorded delivery counter
Tendrá que envolverlo bien	You'll have to wrap it properly

En el banco y en Correos

D i

In the following conversations you will hear five telegrams mentioned. Link the two halves of each telegram below.

a) A brother   i) is very seriously ill.
b) A father   ii) cannot come to the wedding.
c) An aunt   iii) has had an accident.
d) A cousin   iv) sends congratulations on a birth.
e) A friend   v) asks you not to travel.

D ii

You will hear somebody asking you in Spanish to send two telegrams in English to a friend in England.

Look at the telegram form below, listen to the instructions and write the telegrams, giving the details asked for on the form.

EL EXPEDIDOR DEBE RELLENAR ESTE IMPRESO, EXCEPTO LOS RECUADROS EN TINTA ROJA
SE RUEGA ESCRIBA CON LETRAS MAYUSCULAS O CARACTERES DE IMPRENTA

T.G.-1

C.I.F. S-28-16009-C

INS. O NUMERO DE MARCACION	SERIAL	Nº DE ORIGEN	TASA	I.V.A.	TOTAL	INDICACIONES TRANSMISION
	LINEA PILOTO			TELEGRAMA		
OFICINA DE ORIGEN		PALABRAS	DIA	HORA	IMPORTE EN PESETAS	

INDICACIONES: ....

DESTINATARIO: ....
SEÑAS: ....
TELEFONO: ....   TELEX: ....
DESTINO: ....

TEXTO: ....

....

....

....

....

....

| SEÑAS DEL EXPEDIDOR | NOMBRE: .... | TFNO.: .... |
| | DOMICILIO: .... | POBLACION: .... |

UNE A-5 (148 x 210)

Por teléfono

A i Before you listen

A ii

(speech bubbles in photo)
— Hola, ¿qué tal estás?
— Hola, Martyn Soy yo, Rosa

Rosa and Martyn have not seen each other for some time. Rosa is in Spain and Martyn in the UK.

1. Who is making the call, Rosa or Martyn?
2. What are they saying?
3. Invent and practise a possible continuation to the conversation.

Compare your results with the tape (Aii).

Listen and then answer the following questions.

1. When did Rosa telephone before?
2. Where was Martyn when she phoned?
3. What is the weather like in London?
4. What is the weather like in Spain?
5. They talk about two other things. What are they?

A iii

You will hear four short telephone conversations. Write the number of each conversation in the appropriate boxes below

a) speaking ☐
b) not in ☐
c) just a moment ☐
d) wrong number ☐

A iv**

Michael is staying with a Spanish family. While the family is out the telephone rings on three occasions. In each case Michael is asked to take a message. Write down each message in Spanish and then translate it into English.

A v Role play

In pairs, take the parts of A and B in the following role plays.

1   A: Answer the phone.
    B: Ask to speak to A's friend.
    A: Tell him/her that the friend is out but will be back later.
       Ask if he/she wants to leave a message.
    B: Ask A's friend to ring back.
    A: Ask for the number.
    B: Give the number.

2   B: Answer the telephone.
    A: Ask to speak to a friend (Luisa).
    B: Say that Luisa doesn't live here any more.
    A: Ask for her new phone number.
    B: She has no phone.
    A: Ask for the address.
    B: Give the address (Calle Mayor, 27).

A vi Role play**

In pairs take the parts of A and B in the following role plays.

3**

A: You are on holiday on the Spanish coast. You phone your friend who lives in Madrid. After greeting him/her say where you are staying (near Tarragona), what you are doing and answer any questions he/she asks you. Finally make an arrangement to visit him/her.

B: You live in Madrid. Your friend phones from the coast. Ask him/her how he/she is, what he/she is doing and what the weather is like. When he/she asks to visit you tell him/her that you will be away next week but are returning the following week and would like to see him/her.

4**

A: On your way to visit a friend you arrive at the airport earlier than expected. Phone your friend and tell him/her that you will make your own way to his/her house. If he/she insists on coming to meet you, try to dissuade him/her. Reach an agreement.

B: Your friend phones you from the airport. He/she has arrived earlier than expected. He/she insists on finding his/her own way to your house. Try to persuade him/her to let you go to the airport. Reach an agreement.

vocabulary A

Dígame	Hello (telephone. Lit: speak to me.)
¿Está Javier?	Is Javier there?
¿Puedo hablar con Rosa?	Can I speak to Rosa?
Sí, espere un momento	Yes, wait a moment
Ahora se pone	He/she is just coming
¿Quién llama?	Who's calling?
¿Quién es?	Who is it?
No está	He/she isn't here
Ha salido	He/she has gone out
Acaba de salir	He/she has just gone out
No es aquí	Wrong number (Lit: It isn't here)
Se ha equivocado de número	You've got the wrong number
Perdone	I'm sorry
¿Quiere dejar un recado?	Do you want to leave a message?
¿Puedo dejar un recado?	Can I leave a message?
¿De parte de quién?	Who's calling? (lit: On behalf of whom?)
De parte de Alicia	From Alicia
Lo apunto	I'll make a note of it
Dile/Dígale que me llame	Tell him/her to ring me
...cuando vuelva	...when he/she returns
Se lo diré sin falta	I'll tell him/her without fail
Soy yo	It's me (on the telephone)
Soy Yolanda	This is Yolanda
¿Qué tal estás?	How are you?
No contesta	There's no answer
Tengo ganas de ir	I'm looking forward to going
¿Qué tiempo hace?	What's the weather like?
Hace frío/calor	It's cold/hot
Hace mucho viento	It's very windy
Hace un tiempo horrible	It's horrible weather
Llueve	It's raining

Por teléfono

Bi

You will hear eight short extracts from the Spanish telephone information service, which are numbered 1 to 8.

Complete each box with the appropriate number as you listen. The first is done for you.

a) POLICE
b) THE WEATHER
c) TIME
d) NEWS FROM 'RADIO NACIONAL' | 1 |
e) SPORTS NEWS
f) ROADS
g) PROVINCIAL INFORMATION
h) AIRPORT

B ii**

You will hear extracts from the Spanish telephone weather information service. The first part tells you what the weather has been like for the last 24 hours and the second part deals with the weather for today. Complete the weather picture for the various regions.

	The last 24 hours	The next 24 hours
Galicia		
Castilla la Mancha		
Aragón		
Cataluña		
Andalucía		
Las Canarias		

Weather: warm, hot, very hot, cold, very cold, cloudy, rain, stormy, windy, foggy

vocabulary B

el tiempo	the weather (forecast)	El viento sopla fuerte/ moderado	The wind blows strongly/ moderately
nubosidad (f)	cloudy weather	un predóminio del buen tiempo	a predominance of good weather
variable	changeable	nieblas matinales (f)	morning fog
Hay tormentas	There are storms	aumento de las temperaturas	a rise in temperature
puntos (de Galicia)	parts (of Galicia)		
La temperatura fue suave	The temperature was mild		
alta	high		

Oiga, por favor

B iii

Listen to the minimum temperatures for yesterday at various points in Spain. Write the temperatures next to the names of the towns on the map below.

C i

You will hear 6 times given by the telephone clock. What are they?

1 _____   4 _____
2 _____   5 _____
3 _____   6 _____

D i

You will hear five extracts of sports information (**Información Deportiva**). For each of the extracts write down the name of the sport.

1 _____
2 _____
3 _____
4 _____
5 _____

B iv Speaking

In pairs, discuss the weather in the different seasons of your own country. Does it vary in different parts of the country?
Practise the questions:

¿Qué tiempo hace en invierno?
                    verano?
                    primavera
                    otoño?

D ii**

Now listen to Di again and give further details of each item of sports news

1 _____
2 _____
3 _____
4 _____
5 _____

LLAMADAS A TRAVES DE OPERADORA

Por teléfono

E i

In the following 3 dialogues the caller is asking to make a reverse charge call (**una llamada a cobro revertido**) or is ringing through the operator. Write down the number required and the caller's number in each case.

	Number required	Caller's number
1		
2		
3		

E ii Role play

Now practise similar dialogues in pairs. The numbers are supplied below. The first number is the caller's and the second is the number required.

1 29 79 92 / 788 8562 (Barcelona)
2 32 65 76 / 588 4429 (Madrid)
3 636 1867 / 720 8342 (Bilbao)
4 42 24 57 / 692 3409 (Sevilla)

E iii**

In each of the following 5 conversations, the operator has either failed to make the connection requested or has made the connection and is speaking to that person. Add the appropriate number to each of the boxes below.

a) No answer ☐
b) Line engaged ☐
c) The lines are busy ☐
d) Will you accept the call? ☐
e) The line is dead. Are you sure it's the right number? ☐

E iv

You need to phone people in several cities in Spain. You have just phoned the operator and have given her the list of towns you want to contact. You will hear her giving you the code numbers. Look at the map below and add the correct telephone code to each city mentioned.

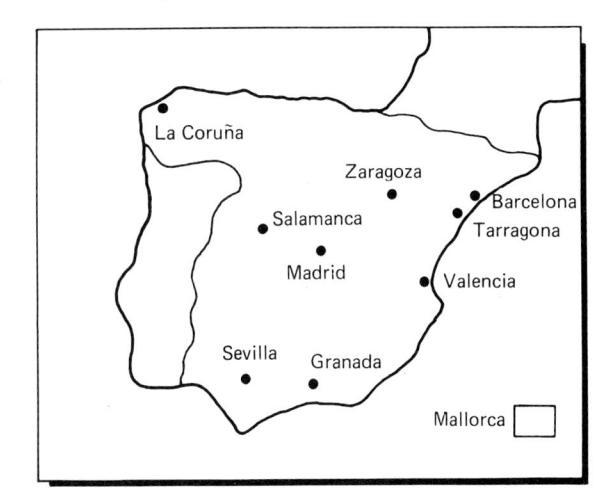

[Map of Spain showing: La Coruña, Zaragoza, Barcelona, Salamanca, Tarragona, Madrid, Valencia, Sevilla, Granada, Mallorca ☐]

---

vocabulary E

Quiero/Quisiera hacer una llamada a cobro revertido	I'd like to make a reverse charge call	No cuelgue	Don't hang up
¿Podrá ponerme con el 65 de Azuara?	Could you connect me with Azuara 65?	Ahora le pongo	I'm putting you through
¿Cuál es su número?	What is your number?	¿Acepta la llamada?	Do you accept the call?
¿A qué número llama?	What number are you ringing?	Está comunicando	It's engaged
¿Con qué número quiere hablar?	Which number do you want to speak to	Las líneas están ocupadas.	The lines are all busy
		marcar	to dial
		prefijo	code

En la comisaría 12

A i Before you listen

"Me han robado el bolso."
"¿Qué le pasa?"

What is the policewoman's question?
What is the woman telling her?
What other questions will the policewoman ask?
What answers might the woman give? (In Spanish)

A ii

Now listen to the woman reporting a theft. What do you learn about the stolen bag?

1 Where was it stolen?
2 Who was the woman with?
3 Who stole it?
4 When was it stolen?
5 What other details can you remember?

A iii

Look at the pictures of the three bags below and decide which one she is describing. Listen to the tape again to help you.

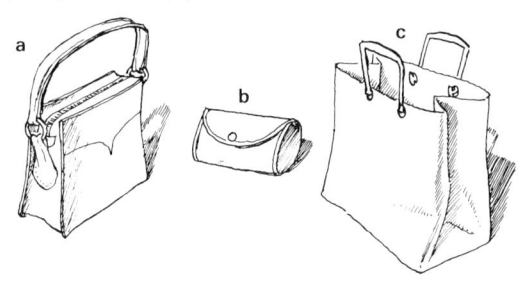

A iv

Seven of the objects you see below were in the woman's bag. Tick each of the seven. The first is done for you. Do you know the names of the objects that were *not* in the bag?

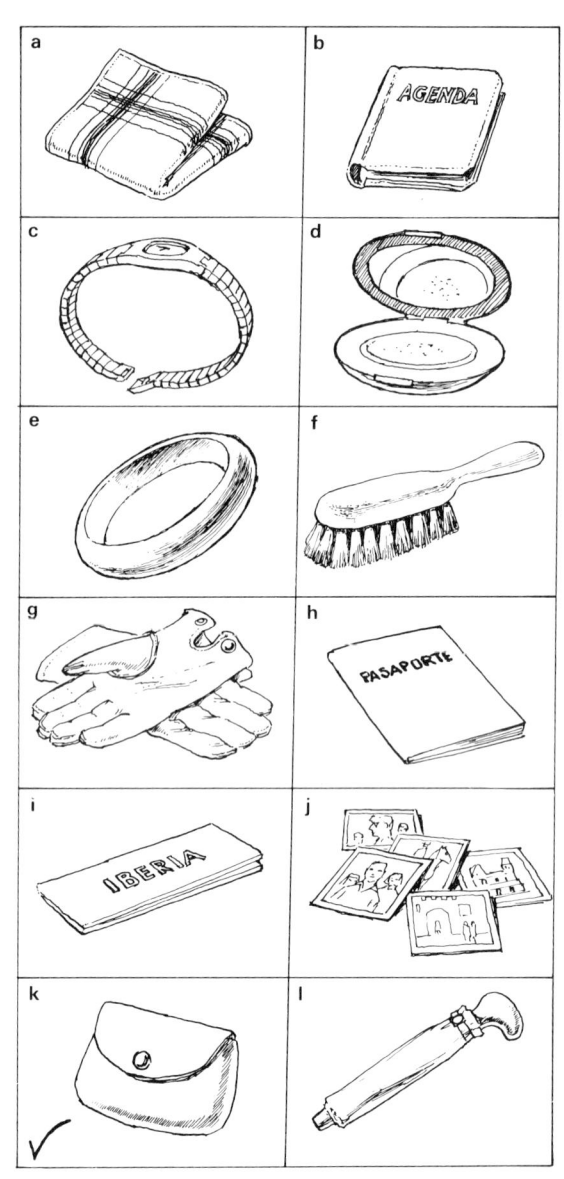

En la comisaría

A v

Look at the details of five similar thefts. On the tape you will hear *three* of these reported to the police. Indicate which three. The events are not always in the same order.

```
Time:   10 am                                a
Place:  Shop entrance
What:   Wallet (plastic)
How:    Taken from pocket
Who:    Doesn't know
```

```
Time:   10 pm                                b
Place:  A bar
What:   A leather handbag
How:    Taken from chair
Who:    Two men
```

```
Time:   11 am                                c
Place:  Street
What:   Purse
How:    Taken from bag
Who:    Young man
```

```
Time:   10.30 am                             d
Place:  Restaurant
What:   Purse
How:    Taken from pocket
Who:    Not sure
```

```
Time:   11 am                                e
Place:  On a bus
What:   Wallet (leather)
How:    Taken from handbag
Who:    Doesn't know
```

A vi** Role play (A)

Which of the incidents in Av are *not* mentioned in the tape? In pairs act out similar dialogues for these two using the information to help you.

Role play (B)

In pairs act out a dialogue at the police station; A is reporting the missing item, B is the police officer.

A: You have lost your bag on a bus.
B: Ask at what time.
A: At about 3 pm.
B: Ask what it's like.
A: It's a big blue leather bag.

Now invent another similar dialogue.

A vii

En la oficina de objetos perdidos.

Look at the objects in Aiv again.
In the three dialogues you will hear a person enquiring about something he/she has lost. Decide which of the articles in Aiv is being referred to, complete the details below and indicate whether it has been found or not.

1   Object: gloves
    Colour: _____
    Material: _____
    Where lost: _____
    Found?:   yes

2   Object: _____
    Colour: _____
    Material: _____
    Where lost: _____
    Found?:   _____

Oiga, por favor

3 Object: _____
   Colour: _____
   Material: _____
   Where lost: _____
   Found?: _____

vocabulary A

Quiero denunciar un robo	I want to report a robbery/theft	Estaba en un bar	I was in a bar
Me han robado el bolso	My bag has been stolen	en la barra	at the bar
Me han quitado el monedero	My purse has been stolen	la entrada de una tienda	the entrance of a shop
		¿Puede describirlo/la/los/las?	Can you describe it/them?
		¿Cómo es?	What's it like?
He perdido la cartera	I've lost my wallet	¿Qué llevaba?	What did it contain?
unos guantes	some gloves	¿Qué había dentro?	What was inside?
un anillo de oro	a gold ring	Es bastante grande	It's quite big
un paraguas azul	a blue umbrella	oscuro	dark
Me lo/la he dejado …	I left it … .	una cremallera	a zip
devolver	to give back	Es de piel	It's made of leather
¿Lo ha devuelto?	Has he/she given it back?	plástico	plastic
Alguien se lo/la llevó	Someone took it	Había …	There was …
Alguien lo/la cogió de mi bolsillo	Someone took it from my pocket	Llevaba …	It had (in it) …
		un pañuelo	a handkerchief
Desapareció sin darme cuenta	It disappeared without me realising	una agenda	a diary
		unas fotos	some photographs
¿Cuándo ha ocurrido?	When did it happen?	un cepillo	a brush
¿A qué hora ocurrió?	What time did it happen?	un espejo	a mirror
¿Dónde …?	Where …?	dinero (m)	money
¿Cómo …?	How?	las llaves	keys
A las doce (más o menos)	(At about) twelve o'clock.	Le avisaremos	We'll let you know.
A eso de las doce	At about twelve o'clock.		

B i

Listen to the news broadcast about a robbery. From the description, decide which *two* of the four boys below took part.

a   b   c   d

B ii

Now look at the pictures of the boys in Bi. Choose either of the boys *not* described in the news broadcast and describe him to your partner. Your partner must guess which one you are describing.

B iii

Now listen to someone describing a person's face. As you listen, draw the face and then compare the result with a partner. Are there any differences between the two drawings? There are two examples.

B iv

Now draw another face and, without showing your partner, describe your drawing to him/her. Your partner must draw the face from your description. Compare with your original drawing.

B v**

Listen to the description of a girl missing from her home. Add the missing details to the police 'missing persons form' below.

B vi Role plays**

Act out, with a partner, the following role plays. In each case, A is a member of the public making a report to the police, and B is the police officer.

1. **A:** You think you have seen the missing girl described in Bv.
   B: 'A' thinks he/she has seen the missing girl in Bv. Ask him/her where, when and ask for a description.

2. **A:** You are on holiday and you are worried because your friend has disappeared. You are speaking to a police officer. You start, then answer the police officer's questions.
   B: 'A' is reporting a missing person. Make notes and ask questions to fill in a similar form to the one in Bv.

3. **A:** Someone stole your bag yesterday as you walked along the street. Describe to the police officer what happened. Describe the bag, its contents and the thief.
   B: 'A' is reporting a robbery. Ask questions about the bag, its contents and the thief. Take notes.

PERSONA DESAPARECIDA

Nombre: __MARÍA PÉREZ GARCÍA__

Sexo: __H__

Edad: _____

Descripción física: _____

_____

Vestida: _____

_____

_____

Rasgos especiales: _____

Oiga, por favor

vocabulary B

Se cometió un robo	A robbery was committed	Lleva barba/bigote	He has a beard/moustache
amenazar	to threaten	Lleva pendientes	He/she is wearing earrings
una navaja	a knife	Llevaba . . .	He/she was wearing . . .
Es/Era moreno/a	He/she is/was dark	Viste/Vestía . . .	He/she was dressed in . . .
alto/a	tall	jersey de lana (*m*)	a woollen jersey
delgado/a	thin	falda (*f*)	a skirt
de estatura media	of medium build	camiseta blanca (*f*)	a white shirt
de mediana altura	of medium height	pantalones de pana (*m*)	cord trousers
ni gordo ni bajo	neither fat nor thin	zapatos (*m*)	shoes
joven	young	vaqueros (*m*)	jeans
mayor	old	gafas (de montura metálica) (*f*)	(metal-framed) glasses
pelirrojo/a	red-haired		
Tiene pelo rizado	He/she has curly hair	gafas redondas/cuadradas (*f*)	round/square glasses
Tenía pelo liso	He/she had straight hair		
largo	long	Aparenta más edad	He/she looks older
corto	short	Está muy desarrollada	She is well-developed
las orejas grandes	big ears	dirigirse a la emisora	contact the radio station
una nariz ancha/recta/larga	a wide/straight/long nose	El puesto de la policía	the police station
ojos pequeños	small eyes		

C i**

Look at the five headlines below from a local newspaper. What do you think the accompanying articles will be about? What do you want to know about the stories?

C ii**

Listen to the five items of news from a local radio station. Match each item (numbered below) with a letter from Ci.

1 ____   4 ____
2 ____   5 ____
3 ____

a Un tirón que acabó en muerte

b Un grave accidente en la Carretera de Huesca

c Detenidos dos traficantes de cocaina

d Cinco quemados por una explosión de butano

e Un atraco frustrado a un banco

En la comisaría

📼 C iii**

Now listen to the same news items again. In English, describe briefly what happened in each. The guidelines below will help you.

1. How many people were involved?
   What happened to the car?
   _____

2. How many people were involved?
   What happened to the victim?
   _____

3. How many people were injured?
   What happened?
   _____

4. How many people were involved?
   Why were they arrested?
   _____

5. How many men were there?
   Why did they leave with no money?
   _____

📼 D i**

You will hear part of an information programme from the radio in which someone is describing a special brochure designed to help tourists in Spain. Answer the questions below.

1. What is the main aim of the brochure?
2. How much does it cost?
3. How many copies have been printed?
4. The brochure has been produced in several languages.
   a) How many?
   b) What are they?
5. Three recommendations are mentioned from the brochure. What are they?
6. Three suggested precautions are mentioned from the brochure. What are they?

79

En el médico y la farmacia

A i Before you listen

Me duele la garganta

¿Qué te pasa?

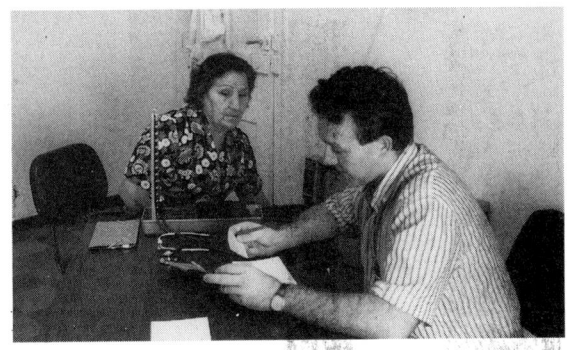

What are Gustavo's symptoms? What will the doctor give him? What advice will he give him?

What other reasons are there for going to the doctor?

Practise describing symptoms in Spanish.

Symptoms

sore eyes ☐
stomach ache ☐
earache ☐
temperature ☐
sore back ☐
diarrhoea ☐
headaches ☐
fainting ☐

A ii

You will hear the conversation between the doctor and Gustavo. Write down the following:

1. Two of his symptoms.
2. How long he has had the symptoms.
3. The doctor's diagnosis.
4. The doctor's prescription.
5. Two pieces of advice.

Illness

swollen tonsils ☐
food poisoning ☐
indigestion ☐
ear infection ☐
sunstroke ☐
flu ☐
chest infection ☐

A iii**

You will hear three dialogues (nos. 1, 2 and 3) which take place in a doctor's surgery.

In each dialogue *some* (not all) of the symptoms and illnesses listed opposite are mentioned. Write the appropriate dialogue numbers in the boxes. Remember – you will not use all the boxes.

A iv**

Now look at the five prescriptions on page 81. Listen to the dialogues in Aiii again. Three of the prescriptions are referred to on the tape. Indicate which three.

Note cards:

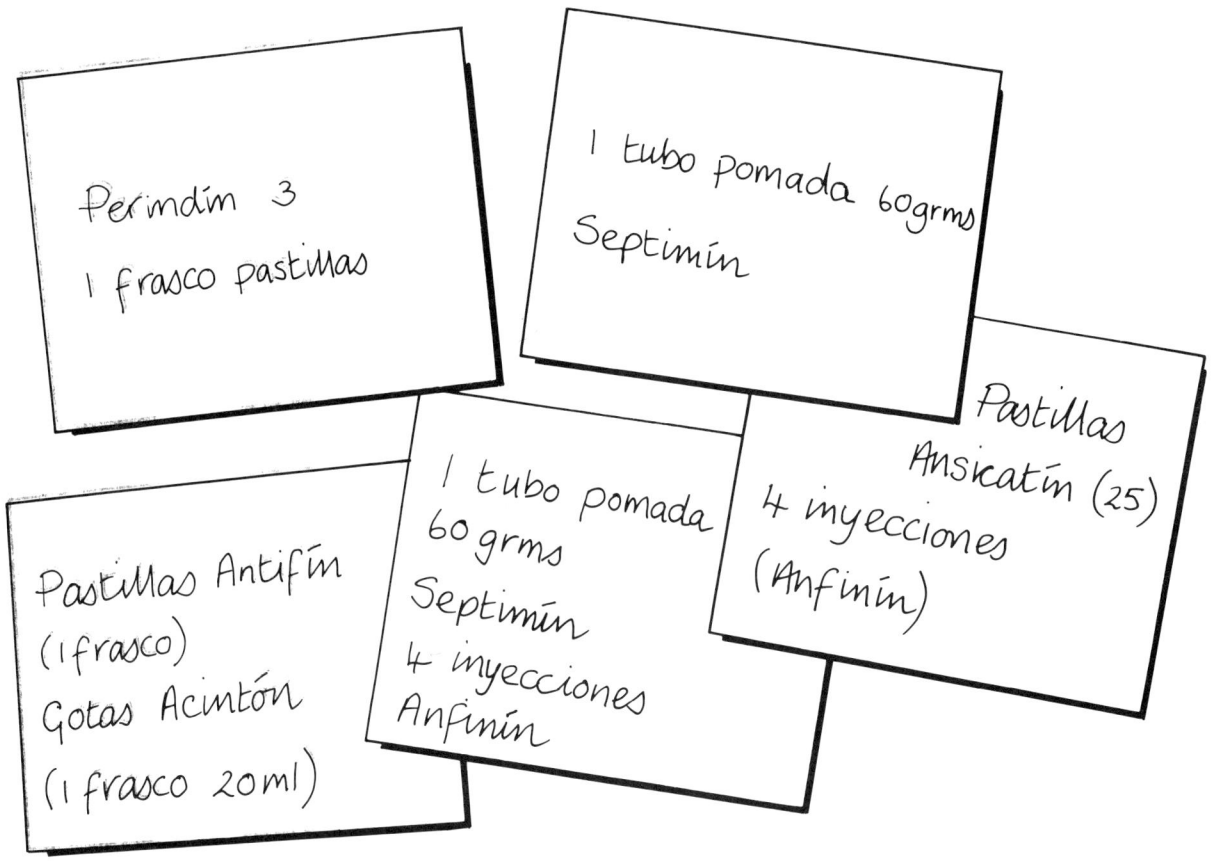

- Perindín 3
  1 frasco pastillas

- 1 tubo pomada 60 grms
  Septimín

- Pastillas Antifín
  (1 frasco)
  Gotas Acintón
  (1 frasco 20ml)

- 1 tubo pomada
  60 grms
  Septimín
  4 inyecciones
  Anfinín

- Pastillas
  Ansicatín (25)
  4 inyecciones
  (Anfinín)

vocabulary A

¿Qué te/le pasa?	What's the matter with you?
Me duele la garganta/la cabeza	My throat/my head hurts
Tengo dolor de estómago	I've got stomach ache
Tengo hinchado el oído	My ear is swollen
el pie	my foot
Me escuece (escocer)	It stings (burns) me
Me escuece la espalda	My back stings (burns)
los hombros	my shoulders
Tengo fiebre	I've got a temperature
tos (f)	a cough
gripe (f)	flu
catarro (m)	a cold
una infección	an infection
intoxicación (f)	food poisoning
diarrea (f)	diarrhoea
insolación (f)	sunstroke
Estoy/me siento	I am/I feel . . .
bien	well
mal	bad
mejor	better
peor	worse
mareado/a	faint
sano	healthy
enfermo/a	ill
Estoy a régimen	I'm on a diet
Llevo dos días así	I've been like this for two days
Toma/Tome estas pastillas	Take these pills
Ponte/Póngase/esta pomada/estas gotas	Apply this ointment/these drops
No vayas a la piscina	Don't go to the swimming pool
No tome(s) el sol	Don't sunbathe
No se bañe/No te bañes	Don't bathe
No se moje/No te mojes	Don't get wet
recetar	prescribe
receta	prescription
una inyección	an injection
un practicante	medical assistant

Oiga, por favor

A v Role play

Take the parts of the doctor and the patient in the following role plays.

a) *Doctor:* Ask what is the matter.
   Patient: You have stomach ache.
   Doctor: Ask when it started.
   Patient: Two days ago.

Using a similar pattern, substitute the following details:

b) a temperature since yesterday
c) ear ache a week ago
d) headache and eyes hurt since yesterday afternoon

** Continue the conversations. The doctor must ask for more information and finally prescribe treatment and give advice. Use the vocabulary list to help you.

1 a) _____
  b) _____
2 a) _____
  b) _____
  c) _____

Bi En la farmacia

With a partner, write down, in Spanish, a list of things you can buy in a chemist.
  Now listen to the two dialogues and write down the things that each customer buys. Were they on your list?

Bii Role play

In the following role plays take the parts of the customer and the chemist in pairs. The customer starts by saying ¿Tiene algo para . . .?

Customer's symptoms	What the chemist recommends
a) a cough	cough syrup
b) diarrhoea	pills
c) sore eyes	drops

vocabulary B

farmacia	chemist	afonía	loss of voice
¿Tienes algo para . . .?	Have you anything for . . .?	chicle (*m*) sin azúcar	sugar-free chewing gum
mareo	seasickness/carsickness	fresa	strawberry
quemaduras solares	sunburn	menta	mint
quemaduras de escaldado	scalds		
tiritas (cortadas/sin cortar)	plasters (individually cut/in a strip)		

En el medico y la farmacia

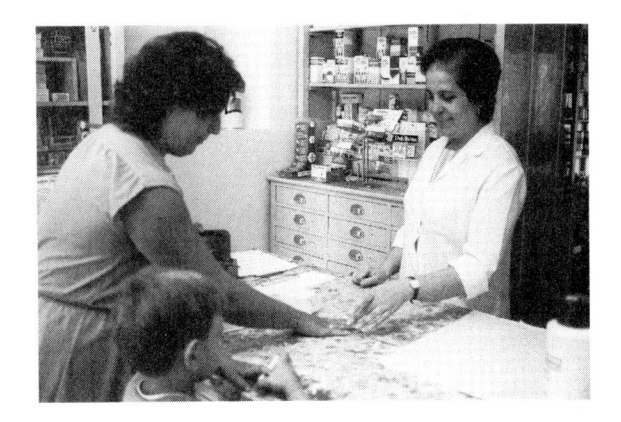

C i

You will hear five short dialogues. Write down where each one takes place. The first is done for you.

1 At reception in a doctor's waiting room
2 _____
3 _____
4 _____
5 _____

C ii**

Now listen to the dialogue again and write down what the people are saying or asking in each one. The first one is done for you.

1 She is making an appointment to see the doctor at 11.
2 _____
3 _____
4 _____
5 _____

C iii Role play

In pairs, act out the following role plays.

1 A: Tell the receptionist you have an appointment at 10.
   B: Ask the patient to wait for a few minutes.

2 A: Your tooth hurts. Ask to make an appointment as soon as possible.
   B: Offer an appointment this afternoon at 5.
   A: Accept

3 A: You have broken your glasses. Ask the optician to repair them.
   B: Say you will repair them immediately.

4 **A: You want to make an appointment for tomorrow to see the dentist.
   B: Tell A that tomorrow is full.
   A: You are going on holiday the next day.
   B: Offer an appointment very early for the day after tomorrow.
   A: Think about it, then either accept it or reject it.

5 **A: You have returned to your doctor after spraining your ankle. Your ankle is much better. Ask if you can take the bandage off.
   B: Advise him/her to keep the bandage on for another week.
   A: You want to know if you can start playing sport again.
   B: Not for another two weeks at least.

Oiga, por favor

vocabulary C

¿Podría darme hora?	Could you give me an appointment	sacar una muela/un diente	to take out a tooth
		empastar (un empaste)	to fill (a filling)
Tengo hora para el médico	I've got an appointment to see the doctor	enfermero/enfermera	nurse
		sala de espera	waiting room
¿Le va bien mañana?	Does tomorrow suit you?	visita (del médico)	surgery hours
Pase por aquí	Come this way	planta	floor (in a building)

D i Emergencias

Look at the pictures below. These are the places you can go in Spain if you have an accident or you fall ill suddenly. If you can't wait for an ambulance it is possible to go by car, waving a white handkerchief from the window.

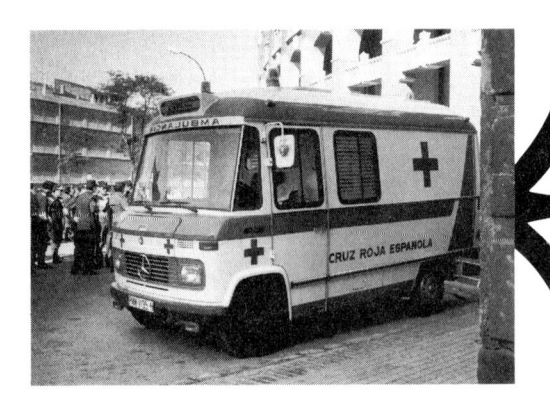

En el medico y la farmacia

D ii

You will hear 7 short statements from people who have just arrived at one of these three places. They are describing their injuries or illnesses.

Look at the picture of the human body below:

a) Put the correct number of the statement in the appropriate box.

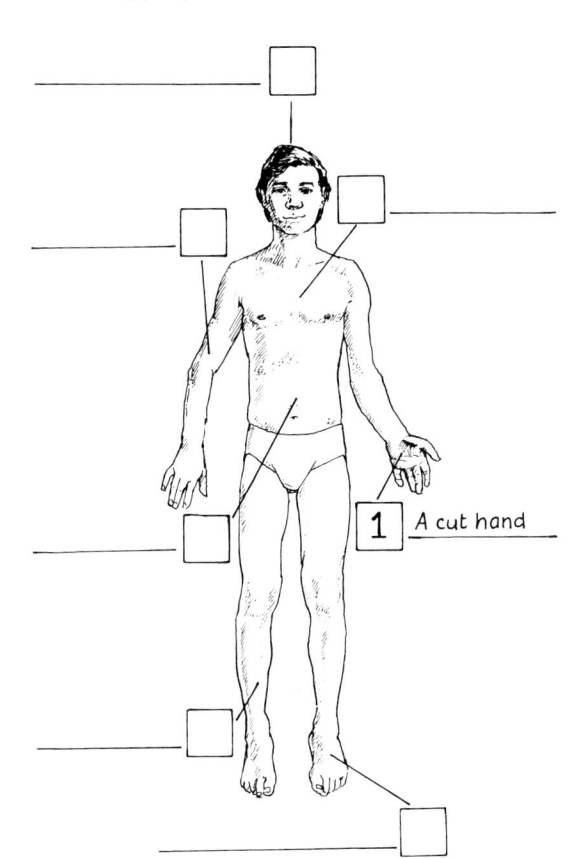

b)** Say *how* each part is affected.

Do part a) first, then listen again to complete part b).

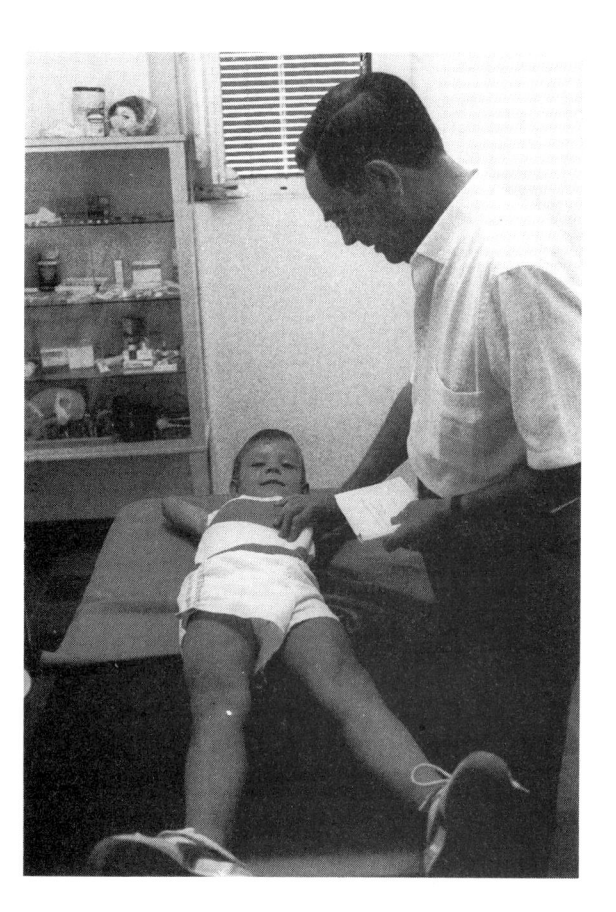

1 A cut hand

vocabulary D

Me he cortado en la mano	I've cut my hand	Me he torcido el tobillo	I've twisted my ankle
Me he quemado	I've burnt myself	Le ha dado un ataque al corazón	He's had a heart attack
Se ha quemado	He/She has burnt him/herself		
la pierna	my leg	Está herido	He/She is injured
Se ha dado un golpe	He/She has bumped him/herself	en el brazo	in the arm
		Ha tenido un accidente (de coche)	He/She has had a (car) accident
Me he caído	I've fallen over (I fell over)	vomitar	to vomit

85

Oiga, por favor

📼 Ei **

You will hear part of a radio programme entitled **'Consejos para el verano'** ('advice for the summer'). Look at the pictures below and indicate what piece of advice is connected with each picture. The first one is done for you.

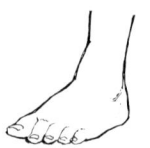

14 La radio y la televisión

The material in this unit is taken from radio and television programmes.

A Presentación de programas

A i

You will hear a television presenter announcing three programmes. Put them in the correct order.

Film. ☐
News ☐
Film for children. ☐

A ii

Now listen again to the description of the *film* and give the following information:

1   The year the film was made.
2   The number of Spanish actors in the film.

A iii**

Describe the story of the film in your own words to your partner or to your teacher.

Oiga, por favor

B Información personal

📼 B i

You will hear the opening part of a television quiz programme. Indicate *True* or *False* for the following statements

1. Carmina is the mother.
2. Sonsoles introduces the family.
3. There are four members of the family appearing on the programme.
4. Sonsoles is in her second year at a nursing college.
5. There are six children in the family altogether.
6. One of the sisters is studying to become a teacher:

C En el instituto.

📼 C i

You will hear the following advertisement from a teacher of EGB on a Spanish phone-in radio programme. You think your friend, with whom you are staying, may be interested. Leave a note for him/her with as many details as possible.

```
Teacher of  E G B




Phone  Isabel :
```

D Tiempo libre

📼 D i

Listen to the opening of '**Tocata**', a television programme, and answer the following questions:

1. How long does it last?
2. What day is it shown?
3. What type of programme is it?
4. Has Rose appeared on the show before?

📼 D ii**

Listen to this description of 'drive-in' cinemas in Spain. Answer the questions:

1. When was the first '**auto-cine**' (drive-in cinema) in Spain?
2. Where was it?
3. Why was it not successful?
4. Where was the second one opened?
5. How long has the 'Star' cinema been open?
6. How many cars will it hold?
7. Is it open all the year round?
8. What do you have to do if you need a waiter/waitress?
9. What is the most popular food served?
10. In the summer what do you receive with your ticket?

📼 D iii

You will hear an announcement describing new sports facilities in a local village. *One* of the following facilities is *not* mentioned. Which one?

a) swimming pool
b) tennis court
c) 'frontón court
d) basketball court
e) handball court

E En el bar y el restaurante

E i**

You will hear part of a radio programme on consumer protection. In it you will hear three pieces of advice or warnings on 'eating out'. What does the presenter say about each of the following?

1. The menu.
2. The bill.
3. Mayonnaise.
4. Food poisoning
5. 'Pinchos' (bar snacks).

D iv

You will hear part of a quiz show in which contestants have to supply the answers to the definitions below.

Can you provide correct answers in Spanish?
Compare your answers with those of your partner and then compare them with the answers on the tape.

1. Algo que las mujeres lleven en el bolso.
2. Un país sin ser España donde se hable castellano.
3. Un medio público de transporte.
4. Algo rojo que se ponga en la ensalada.

F En la ciudad y en la carretera

F i

You will hear two people giving advice on TV. There is one question for each:

1. What is the girl recommending?
2. What does the boy suggest as a good idea for his town?

Oiga, por favor

G El hotel y el apartamento

🎦 G i

Look at the two advertisements below showing flats to let. Listen to the extract from a phone-in radio programme and decide which flat is mentioned first.

> # alquilo piso
>
> *4 habitaciones*
> *cocina/baño nuevos*
> *preferiblemente —*
> *matrimonio joven*

> # se alquila piso
>
> *4 habitaciones*
> *cocina y baño —*
> *nuevas condiciones*
> *— estudiantes*

H En el camping y en la playa

🎦 H i**

You will hear a man and a woman describing the sport of windsurfing. They give four important pieces of advice. What are they?

La radio y la televisión

I Las compras

I i**

Listen to this advertisement for Schweppes and answer the following questions:

1. What is the free gift?
2. How many are they giving away?
3. Are they offering anything else?
4. Where can you find out if you have won a free gift?

I ii

You will hear an advertisement for a large foodstore on a local radio station. The two columns below show the same items but the prices do not match. Rearrange the prices to match the products.

1	dinner plate	a)	199 pts
2	cup and saucer	b)	159 pts
3	serving bowl	c)	135 pts
4	eau de Cologne	d)	399 pts
5	Nivea hand cream	e)	285 pts
6	school sports bag	f)	995 pts
7	track suit	g)	999 pts
8	man's shirt	h)	695 pts
9	ladies' shoes	i)	119 pts

I iii**

Now listen to the second part of the same advertisement. List five items of food on special offer.

1. _____
2. _____
3. _____
4. _____
5. _____

1. _____
2. _____
3. _____
4. _____

H ii

In this extract from the same programme a woman is describing her holidays in the same town. Indicate *True* or *False* for the following statements:

1. She has been coming here for 18 years.
2. She always stays in a hotel.
3. She thinks it is a pretty town.
4. She thinks it is dirty in the summer.
5. Her favourite part is the square.

H iii

Listen to this short advertisement. What type of product is it advertising?

Oiga, por favor

J El teléfono

J i**

Listen to this account of a new telephone card system and answer the following questions:

1 Which two parts of Spain are experimenting with the new system?
2 Where can you buy the cards?
3 How much do they cost?
4 What advantage do they give to the public?
5 Why did the telephone company choose these two areas to carry out the experiment?
6 What advantage do they give the telephone company?

K En la comisaría

K i**

You will hear a description of four items of lost or found property. Look at the list below and indicate which have been lost (L) and which have been found (F).

a) bracelet _____   e) purse _____
b) ring _____   f) watch _____
c) necklace _____   g) money _____
d) key ring _____   h) handbag _____

L En el médico

L i**

In this extract from a programme about health and safety on holiday, you will hear the presenter giving four sets of circumstances when you should not bathe in the sea. What are they?

1 _____
2 _____
3 _____
4 _____
5 How long should you wait after a meal before bathing?

L ii

Listen to the advertisement. What type of product is being advertised?

M i

The last television programme of the evening. What is the date tomorrow? Buenas noches